SAMSUNG

GALAXY A35

USER GUIDE

The Complete Manual For Beginners & Seniors With Instructions On How To Master The Samsung Galaxy A35 5G. With Illustrations, Tips & Tricks

By

Alan McDonald

Table of Contents

INTRODUCTION
Evaluation of the 5G Samsung Galaxy A35

A versatile option that won't break the bank

Nowadays, we commonly find mid-range smartphone options that cater to many distinct but related use cases. For instance, Realme has been attempting to get into the gaming smartphone market with its integrated 3D VC liquid cooling systems, whilst Vivo focuses mostly on phones with cameras. Plus, we think it's better to excel in one thing rather than trying to be good at everything.

But suppose you want something that can do a few different tasks. The newly released Samsung Galaxy A35 5G, however, guarantees just that. After many days of testing, we provide our verdict on the Samsung Galaxy A35 5G.

The 5G Samsung Galaxy A35 style

One may make the case that the Samsung Galaxy A35 looks too much like other high-end S-series phones, such as the Galaxy S23 FE and the Galaxy S24. However, we aren't grumbling about it.

With its high-quality metal body and transparent glass back, the smartphone looks stunning and seems much more expensive than it is. This does add some weight to the phone, however. Even though it's comfortable to carry, if you want a lightweight gadget, you may want to search elsewhere.

Corning Gorilla Glass Vitus and IP67 dust and water resistance shield this stylish phone. However, a cover is necessary due to the phone's protruding camera lenses and the fact that the glass back is very prone to smudges. At the very least, it should be transparent.

Evaluation of the 5G Samsung Galaxy A35

The 5G screen and speakers of the Samsung Galaxy A35

Among organic light-emitting diode screens, Samsung has a reputation for excellence. Like all other FHD+ Super AMOLED displays, the one on the Galaxy A35 5G can handle a 120Hz refresh rate and reach a peak brightness of 1,000 nits.

The phone's screen is a visual feast, with crisp lettering, deep blacks, and vibrant colors—perfect for games like Asphalt 9 on "High" settings or watching Kim's Convenience episodes. While some users may find it difficult to reach the screen's edges with a single hand, the 6.6-inch display is otherwise straightforward to use.

Among the better ones we've seen is the phone's twin stereo-speaker configuration. The bass is tight, the highs are distinct, and the sound remains undisturbed even when cranking up the volume.

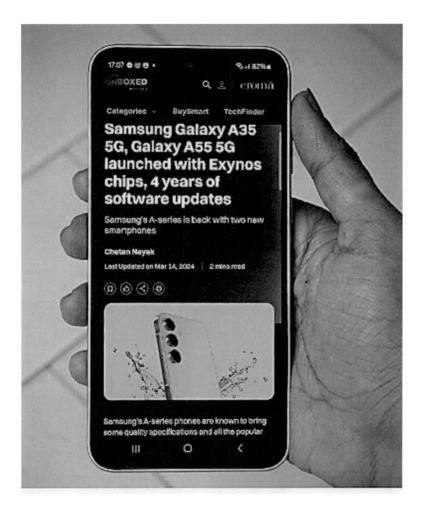

Galaxy A35 5G from Samsung: How it Performs

The Exynos 1380 chipset and Mali-G68 MP5 GPU are Samsung's internal creations. With 8 GB of RAM, you can run numerous programs smoothly and this is more than enough for most typical use scenarios.

The phone never once struggled to keep all of our apps running well, including Google Chrome, the Phone app, Netflix, and even a little Instagram.

What about gaming performance? Call of Duty Mobile and Asphalt 9 operate quite well on this phone at high graphics settings. We didn't see any significant frame rate reductions when playing Asphalt 9, however, there were moments when it felt like hit-or-miss.

Secondly, while playing games on high graphics settings, the phone does become a little hot. Still, it doesn't do anything worrisome.

5G battery for the Samsung Galaxy A35

An impressive 5,000mAh Li-Ion battery powers the Samsung Galaxy A35 5G. We played games and watched Netflix for three hours straight, with an hour of shooting and some heavy torch use thrown in for good measure. The Samsung Galaxy A35 5G still had around 65% battery life even after this, with location services, Wi-Fi, and Bluetooth always enabled (we linked the phones to a set of One Plus Buds Z2).

Most users will find that the phone comfortably lasts all day thanks to its good battery management. The phone's compatibility for 25W wired charging was a little disappointing, however. On top of that, unlike many of its competitors in the same price range, it does not come with an adaptor.

5G cameras on the Samsung Galaxy A35

The primary camera system of the Samsung Galaxy A35 5G is quite powerful. Capturing the finer details on most objects and excelling in low light circumstances are made possible by its 50MP main sensor, 8MP ultra-wide-angle sensor, and 5MP macro sensor.

Images are never noisy or overexposed, even when shot in well-lit outdoor locations. The phone's color reproduction is very acceptable. Still, there are occasions when the pictures could seem a little too saturated for some.

When it comes to portraiture, the camera captures details well, with sharp edges on people and objects alike. The camera seems to have a little more of a soft focus effect on certain objects than we would have liked, however.

Moving on to the videos. The Samsung Galaxy A35 5G produces excellent video quality. Capturing scenes with a lot of action, such as moving traffic on a road, is a piece of cake when using the OIS.

So, using these cameras, you can practice your amateur photography skills and make sure your Instagram is (mainly) great!

Review of the Samsung Galaxy A35 5G Unboxed: Is It Worth It?

When it comes to features and value, the Samsung Galaxy A35 5G is hard to beat. The phone's display, speakers, and cameras are all top-notch, and it runs games well (except for the rare overheating).

Naturally, if you're in the market for a phone with quicker charging capabilities, you may want to check out the Redmi Note 13 Pro and Pro+, which provide a slightly better camera, or the OnePlus Nord CE4.

The Samsung Galaxy A35 5G, on the other hand, is a very powerful smartphone. If you're in the market for a versatile smartphone that won't break the bank but can handle a whole lot, this is a fantastic pick.

CHAPTER ONE

HOW TO START YOUR GALAXY DEVICE IN SAFE MODE

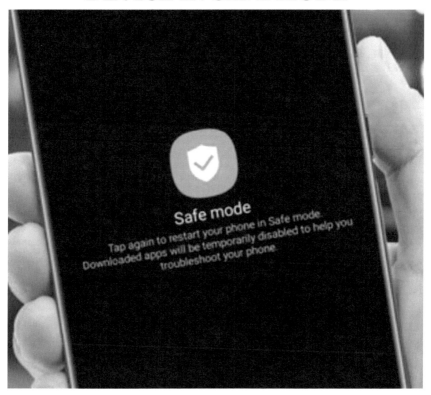

Displaying Safe mode on a Galaxy

A third-party app could be to blame if your mobile device is acting up. Using the Safe mode function might help you identify which app is behaving strangely. You can't install any third-party applications on your smartphone while it's in safe mode. By doing so, you may quickly determine which software is causing the issue and uninstall it.

Depending on your wireless provider, software version, and device type, the screens and options that are available to you may differ.

Launch the device into safe mode.

Important: Some of your personalization settings (wallpapers, themes, etc.) may be restored to factory settings when you leave Safe mode.

1. Turn off your phone and then enter safe mode.
2. Turn off your mobile device entirely first.
3. Once the Samsung logo displays, press and hold the volume down button to power on the device.
4. "Safe mode" should appear in the screen's lower left corner if you've done everything right. Proceed as before if "Safe mode" still does not show up.
5. You may uninstall the problematic third-party program after entering Safe Mode.

To begin, uninstall any applications that had updates or new installations made at the time the issue arose.

If you want to go out of Safe Mode, just restart your device. Alternatively, you may access Safe Mode by tapping the notice that appears when you slide down from the top of the screen. Press the "Turn off" button.

Get into safe mode by going to the Power menu.

If you're still experiencing problems after following the instructions above, you may also access the Power menu and activate Safe mode there.

1. To begin, hit and hold both the side button and the volume down button simultaneously. Alternately, you may use two fingers to swipe down from the top of the screen, and then touch the power symbol.
2. To turn off the power, press and hold the symbol.
3. Press the symbol for Safe mode.

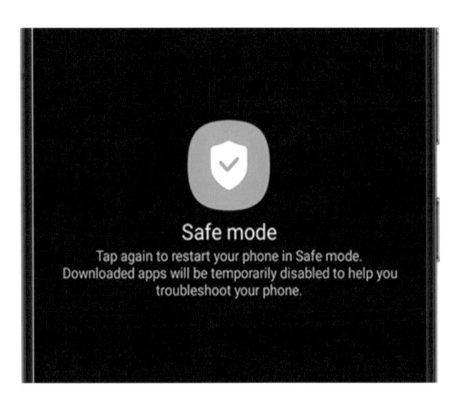

Galaxy phones show safe mode.

4. You may uninstall the problematic third-party program after entering Safe Mode. To begin, uninstall any applications that had updates or new installations made at the time the issue arose.

5. If you want to go out of Safe Mode, just restart your device. Alternatively, you may access Safe Mode by tapping the notice that appears when you slide down from the top of the screen. Press the "Turn off" button.

HOW TO INSERT AND REMOVE MEMORY CARDS

The ability to use SIM and memory cards with your Galaxy handset is device-specific. Newer smartphones and tablets that are compatible with 4G use nano-SIM cards, and the maximum capacity of these cards varies from model to model.

Looking at the sides of your device can help you discover the SIM and memory card slots; however, their exact locations may vary by model.

Be careful not to harm any data saved on a memory card by taking it out of its slot before use.

Plugging in a SIM or SD card

Whatever kind of SIM or memory card you have, you may insert it following these procedures. To avoid damaging or jamming the card in your device, check the card's dimensions before inserting a SIM or memory card.

Items that need a constant power source

1. An ejector PIN should have been included in the packaging of your new gadget. Carefully insert the pin into the SIM tray's hole. The system will open the SIM card.

2. Check out the platter. You may use either two SIM cards or one SIM and an SD card in the dual SIM tray shown in the picture below.

   If you look closely enough at the marks and symbols on your SIM tray—which may vary from model to model—you should be able to discern the proper placement of each card. A memory card or two SIM cards may not work on all devices.

The SIM tray that comes with the S21 models is all new, and it can hold two SIM cards—one on the front and one on the rear.

3. Set the SIM or memory card in the tray so that the contacts that are gold in color are facing down.

Contact your network operator for further help if your SIM card does not fit into your SIM tray properly.

4. Return the tray to your device by gently pushing it in. After proper installation, it should rest flat against your device.

Tools that have a detachable power source

1. Remove the device's rear cover. To facilitate this, a release latch is located on the side.

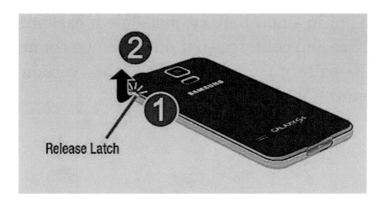

Release Latch

Take the rear cover off.

2. Take the battery unit out.

3. Gently insert your SIM or microSD card into the device's top slot.

   There is a microSD card slot just above the SD card slot and an SD card slot on the bottom. Use the right slot to ensure success.

In the four slots, place your SIM card or microSD card.

4. To put in a new battery, just slide it back into the device and gently push it down. When connecting the battery to the gadget, be certain the connections line up.

Change the power source

5. Reapply the rear cover on your gadget and, using little pressure, push down on the corners until it snaps into position.

Eliminating a storage or SIM card

You should always unmount a memory card before removing it to avoid damaging it or losing any data. When taking a SIM card out, this step is unnecessary.

Removing an SD card's mount

1. Go to Settings and then choose "Device care" or "Device maintenance."
2. Two-Tap Data Saver
3. Three-Tap SD Card
   Tap the More choices icon (three dots) if you don't see this option. Pick "Storage settings" next. The SD card should now be accessible.
4. Demount

   Next, take the SIM or memory card out of the slot. To insert a SIM or memory card into a device that has a replaceable battery, just follow the methods outlined there.

Eliminating a storage or SIM card

1. The device's packaging will include an ejector PIN. Carefully insert the pin into the SIM tray's hole. Pressing open should do the trick.
2. Take the tray out of the tray slot with care.
3. Take out the SIM or memory card
4. Put the tray back into its slot with care.

Sim card varieties

Most modern smartphones (those released in 2014 and after) utilize nano SIM cards. Before then, micro SIMs were the most common.

A Nano SIM differs from a Micro SIM primarily in the size of the plastic encasing the microprocessor. You may now get a single card from most mobile networks that you can bend or snap to fit your specific needs.

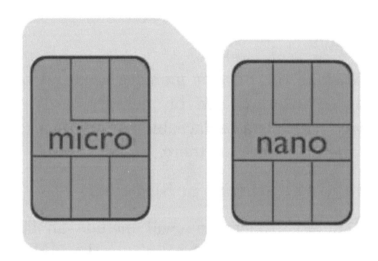

version of sim

Memory card varieties

To add more room to your device's storage, you may use a memory card, often known as an SD card. Secure Digital goes by the initials SD.

SD cards are available in a variety of sizes. There are two main types of SD cards: normal and mini.

Micro SD cards are compatible with the majority of smartphones and tablets that provide additional storage capacity.

You may get memory cards at any supermarket, online, or from any digital shop. Keep in mind that while purchasing less expensive memory cards could save you money initially, they pose a greater risk of corruption and the loss of your data and photographs.

How are SDHC and SDXC different from one another?

Both Secure Digital High Capacity (SDHC) and Secure Digital Extended Capacity (SDXC) SD cards are available with different levels of storage capacity.

The rate at which pictures may be read and written is called class transfer speed. Class, not SD, SDHC, or SDXC, will determine the transfer speed.

Use the Samsung Members app to submit an error report or ask a question if your Samsung mobile, tablet, or wearable is acting strangely.

Thus, we can examine the situation more closely. The data is stored in an anonym zed form and is only kept for as long as the inquiry lasts.

HOW TO FIND YOUR PHONE'S SETTINGS AND ADJUST THE HOME BUTTON

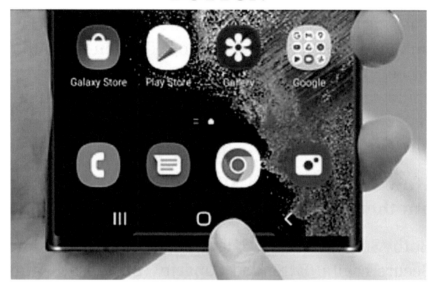

The Home button on most modern phones is an always-on virtual button rather than a physical one. Pressing the Home button will bring up the same menu as pressing any other physical button. No need to fret if you're experiencing problems unlocking your phone or if the Home button seems too touchy. Find out how customizable your phone's Home button is and how to make the necessary adjustments with our help.

Depending on your wireless carrier, software version, and phone type, the screens and options that are available to you may differ.

Oversee the navigation buttons (Home, Back, and Recent).

The placement of the navigation bar's buttons, such as the Back and Recent buttons, is truly customizable!

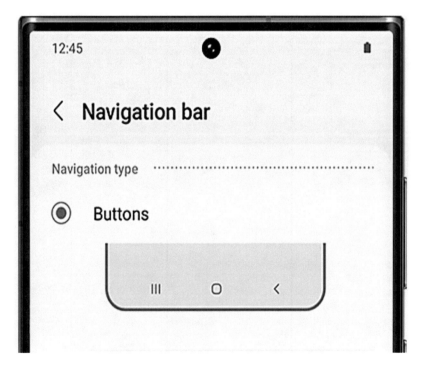

Just go to Settings, and then touch on Display, then finally on the Navigation bar to do this. Pick Buttons from the menu at the top of the screen. Then, at the bottom, you may pick the button arrangement that most suits your needs. The Navigation bar may be arranged in two ways: either following the standard sequence of Recent, Home, and Back, or you can change it to Back, Home, and Recent. There is no method to move the Home button; it remains fixed in the center.

Furthermore, you have the option to replace the conventional buttons on the navigation bar with Swipe motions.

CHAPTER TWO

HOW TO CHARGE YOUR GALAXY DEVICE QUICKLY

You can charge your Galaxy quickly.

The impending or recent demise of your mobile device is not catastrophic. A quick Samsung charger will have it fully charged in no time. If you own a Galaxy, you can charge it quickly, very quickly, or wirelessly. You can buy extra chargers on our website if you ever need them.

Only charge your smartphone using a Samsung-approved device. Your phone or tablet's battery life may be extended with the help of Samsung accessories. Damage and voiding of warranty coverage could result from using third-party accessories.

Keeping the gadget powered

Verify that you are using the appropriate charger for your phone before you begin charging. To charge your phone quickly and efficiently, just follow these three simple steps whenever you're ready.

1. After you've attached your USB cable to your charging adaptor, you may plug it into your phone's USB port.
2. Plugging the adaptor into an electrical outlet is the next step.
   Connecting your adaptor to an electrical outlet will allow it to charge more quickly. You may extend the time it takes to charge by connecting it to a computer or other device via the USB cord.
3. After your phone has completed charging, unplug it from your computer and then unplug the adapter from the wall outlet.

There are a few potential issues that can be preventing your phone from charging. Having said that, you should get a new fast charger if the one you have stops working entirely. You may ask for servicing if it's still covered by the warranty. In such case, we have a new Samsung charger available for purchase on our website.

Lightning-quick, lightning-fast wireless charging

When you need your Galaxy phone or tablet back up and running quickly, you may utilize the fast charging technology included in Samsung chargers. Plus, most phones feature rapid wireless charging. Your phone will activate Fast cable charging the moment you connect it to a Samsung Fast Charger. You may toggle this feature on or off manually; it should be enabled by default.

Only some devices support super rapid charging, and an adapter authorized by Samsung, either 25W or 45W, is required.

1. Start by going to Settings, and then press on Battery to see the charging features.
2. Select Charging settings from the list.
3. Select Quick charging or Quick wireless charging and then tap the corresponding button. Here, only the charging rates that are compatible with your smartphone will be shown. The connected charger and battery state will be used by the device to identify the quickest charging possible.

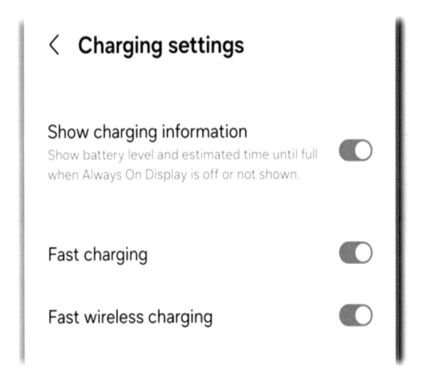

Locate the switch that says "Fast charging" on your Galaxy phone.

4. Simply put the USB power converter into an electrical outlet after connecting the USB cable to your phone or tablet. This will start the rapid charging or super-fast charging process.
Quickly charge your smartphone by placing it on a wireless charger that supports fast charging.

The gadget will give you a quick heads-up when it starts charging, the current speed, and the estimated time to fully charge. Once it has finished charging, it will simply display the remaining time till full.

5. When the battery is completely charged, you may remove the charger from both the device and the outlet.

When connected to a higher-rated charger, your smartphone will automatically choose the fastest charging speed it can handle, even if it doesn't support 45W charging.

HOW TO WIRELESSLY CHARGE REVOLUTION SAMSUNG GALAXY

Keeping in touch is crucial in our fast-paced environment. With their ever-present capabilities for communication, pleasure, and work, mobile phones have become indispensable. The Samsung Galaxy A35 continues Samsung's tradition of being an industry trailblazer in terms of innovation, and it expands the capabilities of smartphones even farther than before. Its ability to charge wirelessly is one of the most remarkable aspects of this remarkable product. What follows is an exploration of wireless charging—what it is, how it works, and why the Samsung Galaxy A35 is the ideal device to use with it.

A History of Charging Innovations

From the first days of mobile devices, charging a phone has gone a long way. When we first started using phones, we plugged them into bulky cable chargers and unplugged them anytime they needed a power boost. Nonetheless, our charging solutions evolved in tandem with technological progress. A major step forward in charging technology's development was the advent of wireless charging.

Wireless Power Distribution Revealed

A game-changer in charging technology, wireless charging does away with the need for wires and plugs altogether. It uses electromagnetic fields instead, which carry power from a charging station to the gadget. Users may charge their gadgets by only putting them on a preset charging pad; this technique is called electromagnetic induction. The Samsung Galaxy A35 makes this state-of-the-art technology more affordable than ever.

How Wireless Charging Works

The basic idea of induction is what allows wireless charging to work. An internal network of wires powers the Samsung Galaxy A35 and the wireless charging pad. An electromagnetic field is created around these coils when an electric current flows through them. The charging station and your Galaxy A35 communicate with one another via their respective coils.

To charge the battery, the phone's coil transforms the electromagnetic energy into electrical energy. Not only is this method very easy to use, but it also reduces the strain on charging ports as physical contact is not required.

Wireless Charging: The Advantages

1. One obvious benefit of wireless charging is how much easier it is to use. Just set your Samsung Galaxy A35 down on a charging mat to get it charged up. In low light, not having to fiddle with cords or connections is a huge help.
2. Decreased Risk of Damage: The conventional way of charging entails physically connecting and disconnecting the gadget, which may cause damage over time. This is no longer an issue with wireless charging, which extends the life of your smartphone.
3. Compatible with Multiple Devices: With wireless charging, you're not confined to only the Samsung Galaxy A35. You'll find this technology supported by a plethora of different devices.

Because of this, you can keep your charging cords tidy by using a single charger for several devices.

4. Enhanced Security: The design of wireless charging stations prioritizes security. You can charge your smartphone securely with features like overcurrent prevention and temperature control.

5. Improved Visual Appeal: Wireless charging provides a more visually pleasant option because there are no visible cords. It may be incorporated into furnishings or even designed into the structure of your house or business.

The Samsung Galaxy A35: A Trailblazer in Wireless Charging?

Wireless charging is used to its most potential by the Samsung Galaxy A35. For those who value practicality and aesthetics, this device's interoperability with wireless charging pads opens up a world of possibilities. Among the many ways in which the Samsung Galaxy A35 breaks new ground in wireless charging is this:

1. Quick and Efficient Wireless Charging: The Galaxy A35 is compatible with rapid wireless charging, so your smartphone will be charged effectively. You can quickly and easily charge

your device with the correct wireless charging pad.

2. The second cutting-edge innovation is Wireless PowerShare, which lets the Galaxy A35 share its battery life with other compatible devices. It's a godsend in times of crisis since it functions similarly to a portable power bank integrated into your smartphone.

3. Wireless Charging Complementary Accessories: The Galaxy A35 is compatible with a variety of wireless charging accessories from Samsung. You may discover the ideal accessory to enhance your charging experience, whether it's a sleek wireless charger or a portable power bank.

4. Samsung Ecosystem Integration: The Galaxy A35 is designed to work in tandem with other Samsung products and services, creating a cohesive ecosystem. This opens up a world of possibilities for controlling your smart home and compatible Samsung appliances from the convenience of your smartphone.

5. The Samsung Galaxy A35's wireless charging feature improves the user experience in general. It's an easy method to keep your smartphone charged, so you can remain connected and get things done all day long.

When it comes to smartphones, the Samsung Galaxy A35 heralds a brand-new age of ease and innovation. For those who priorities practicality and aesthetics, its wireless charging features are a major selling point. Wireless charging is more than a function; it's a way of life that streamlines your everyday tasks and minimizes clutter.

With the widespread use of wireless charging technology, the Samsung Galaxy A35 stands out as a trailblazer in this thrilling development. The Samsung ecosystem is seamlessly integrated, and it delivers a full and pleasurable charging experience with its quick wireless charging and Wireless PowerShare.

HOW TO PERSONALIZE THE GALAXY'S NAVIGATION BAR

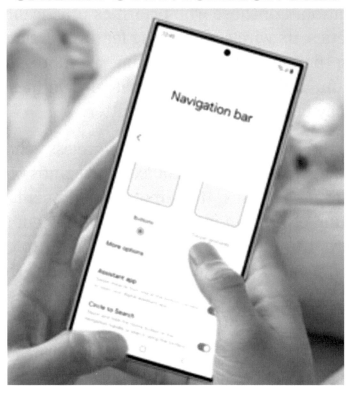

A Galaxy user customizing the navigation bar

At the very bottom of your screen, you'll see the Navigation bar. This is the main menu that allows you to move about your smartphone. But that's not fixed; you can rearrange the Recent, Home, and Back buttons whatever you choose, or even hide them so you can use gestures to navigate your phone.

Depending on your wireless provider, software version, and device type, the screens and options that are available to you may differ.

Click on the menu items to navigate

The three buttons for Recent, Home, and Back are located at the bottom of the screen in the standard Navigation bar. It comes preinstalled on every Galaxy phone and tablet. Descriptions of the three buttons follow:

- On the far left, you'll see the "Recent" button. Your frequently used applications will be shown when you press here.
- Home: The button smack dab in the middle. Pressing this will bring you to the main screen.
- To return, use the button on the far right. To return to the previous screen, tap here.

Certain programs, such as games or video services, have the option to use the whole screen without the navigation bar. To briefly see the bar while using these applications, you may slide up.

Sorting buttons

The Navigation bar's button arrangement is also customizable.

Select Display from the Settings menu, and then choose Navigation bar. Pick Buttons from the menu that appears, and then at the bottom of the screen, you may pick how you want the buttons to be set up.

This setting also controls the starting point of your swipes when utilizing the Swipe motion.

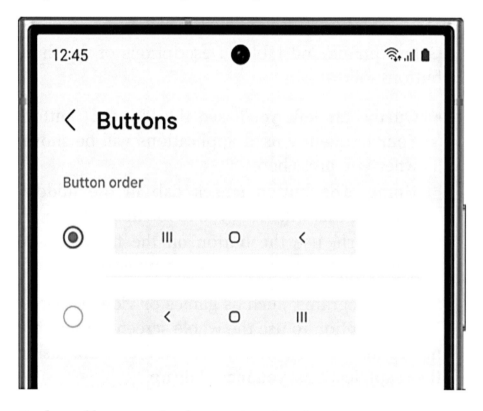

Order of buttons in the navigation bar

Make use of the swipe movements

If you'd rather not use buttons and would want to utilize gestures instead, you may do so. Alternatively, you can even remove the buttons from your screen if you prefer a cleaner design.

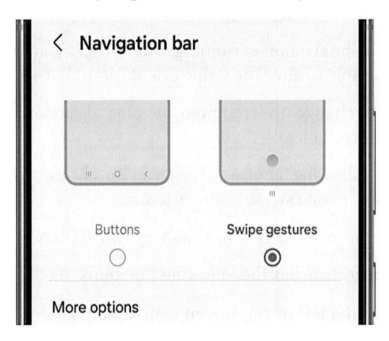

1. Press Display from the Settings menu.
2. Pick Swipe gestures from the menu that appears in the navigation bar.

   One UI 6.1 device does not have gesture suggestions.

3. To get a better idea of where to swipe, use Gesture suggestions. When using Portrait mode, you can access the buttons by hiding the

keyboard, which you can do by turning on the Show button. If you're worried about inadvertently activating a command while sketching or writing, you may use the S Pen to prevent motions.

On smartphones running One UI 6.1, you won't be able to alter the swipe orientation.

4. To change the required swiping direction, tap More choices.

The following choices allow you to choose which Galaxy phone swipe motions to use.

Motions on smartphones running One UI 6.0

Each gesture has the following functions:

- To the left of the screen, you'll see your recently used apps when you swipe up from this location.
- In the middle, you may access the Home screen by swiping up.
- To return to the previous screen, swipe up here (far right).

Hit the option to disable the Gesture hint if you want to hide the Swipe gesture lines entirely. The three lines at the screen's base will vanish.

Touchscreen Interactions with One UI 6.1

- Using a side swipe, install Returns to the screen that was before.
- Scroll from the bottom to the top: Return to the main screen of the app.
- Press and hold to see all the applications that were recently utilized.

Where the Galaxy Z Fold series' navigation bars are located

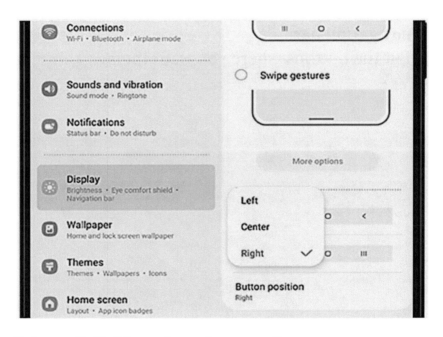

Galaxy Z Fold series phones allow you to center, right-align, or left-shift the navigation bar on the home screen. So, we've got you covered no matter what navigation method you like!

This feature's status determines where the Navigation bar appears. You can only drag the Navigation bar to the left or right on the main screen if it is enabled. With it turned off, the only possible location for the navigation bar is in the middle.

1. To access the display settings, go to the Settings menu.
2. To change the location of a button, touch on the navigation bar.
3. Put the buttons where you want them.

CHAPTER THREE

HOW TO PERSONALIZE THE GALAXY LOCK SCREEN

The Galaxy S24 series has an upgraded version of One UI, which is already common knowledge. New features, including AI-powered tools, were added to Samsung's own Android interface, which also saw some strange alterations to the overall design.

The ability to personalize the lock screen and lock screen widgets on Galaxy devices was altered with the 2022 release of the One UI 5.0 update by

Samsung. The business augmented the settings menu with two sizable visual representations of the lock screen; customers may begin personalizing the lock screen by tapping on one of these icons. Before One UI 6.1, this is how it appeared.

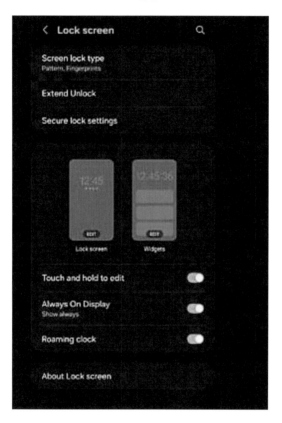

These large "Edit" buttons have been eliminated by Samsung in the latest One UI 6.1 update for the Galaxy S24 series. Strangely, the lock screen customization option is no longer easily accessible. In One UI 6.1, this is how it works.

In One UI 6.1, you may personalize the lock screen.

One UI 6.1's lock screen customization options are limited to the tap-and-hold command. Press and hold to bring up the lock screen, which will lead you to the settings menu.

But you need to have the "Touch and hold to edit" feature turned on for this to function. You could have accidentally disabled this option while importing your settings from an older Galaxy phone if it doesn't function. To restore power:

Navigate to "Lock screen and AOD" in the phone's Settings app, and then turn the "Touch and hold to edit" option to the ON position. Tapping and holding the lock screen now allows you to customize it.

Choose "Edit Lock Screen" from the "Looking for something else? Suggestion box for an additional method to modify the lock screen. Underneath the Lock Screen and AOD menu, you'll see this box. The aforementioned approach remains the only dependable means of accessing lock screen customizations at the moment; however, this recommendation may not be there indefinitely.

HOW TO MANAGE YOUR GALAXY
DEVICE'S NOTIFICATIONS

No worries, we understand that you're preoccupied. Plus, you may not have the time to unlock your device to check and reject all of those alerts while you're in a hurry. Fortunately, your device's notification settings allow you to handle alerts directly from the Lock screen.

Depending on your wireless provider, software version, and device type, the screens and options that are available to you may differ.

Settings for the lock screen's notifications

Notifications, particularly private ones like text messages, are seldom appreciated when others can see them. The good news is that the Lock screen gives you the option to conceal the notification data.

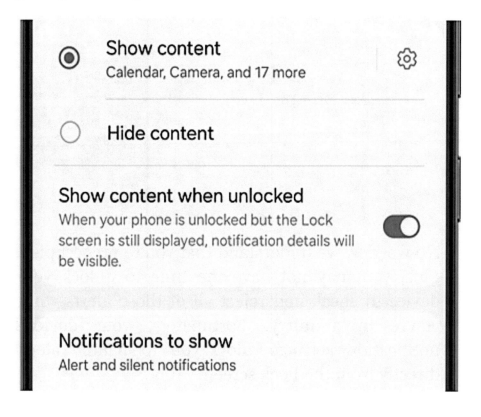

Swipe to the Notifications section of Settings, select it, and then choose Lock screen notifications. To enable lock screen notifications, tap the button located at the top. All of the accessible parameters may be modified from this point:

- Select the option you like for your notifications: hide or show material. Select which applications will display Lock screen alerts by tapping the Settings button after choosing Show content.
- Display content upon unlocking: Unlocking your smartphone will reveal the notification information.
- Indicators seen on the lock screen choose to display the material
- Reminders to display: Choose between alert and quiet alerts or only alerts.

When you're using Always On Display, you may choose to display or conceal alerts. If your device is in power-saving mode, you may not be able to access this option.

Unlock alerts on your lock screen

From your device's Lock screen, you may easily access and dismiss alerts.

To access the Notification panel, double-tap the notification icon on the Lock screen. After that, access the notification you want by tapping on it. If necessary, unlock your phone.

Swipe left or right on the notice you want to dismiss until it goes away.

Secure interface with symbols for notifications

You may be prompted to input your credentials to see the notification if you have activated the screen lock.

Put alerts on snooze

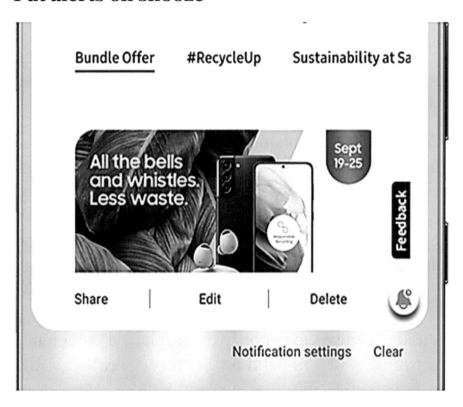

You may "snooze" your alerts in the same way you snooze your alarm clock in the morning. This will cause them to vanish for a certain period before reappearing at the specified time.

From the Lock screen, you may snooze notifications by tapping the down arrow to open them completely.

Select the length of time you would want to set the alarm for, then press the Snooze symbol (which resembles a bell).

A message with the option to snooze and access settings on the left

Some software versions may not have the Snooze function. You may have to go into the preferences and find the snooze option to turn it on. Find Advanced Settings in the Settings menu. Next, hit Notifications. Toggle the Show snooze button on and off.

Notifications of emergency

Public agencies may notify the public via emergency warnings of impending severe weather, the whereabouts of missing individuals, or other situations of regional or national significance. You have the option to personalize your emergency notifications by enabling or disabling certain ones. The only exception to this is the national alerts.

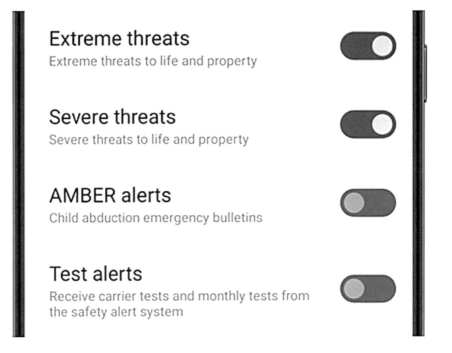

Extreme threats
Extreme threats to life and property

Severe threats
Severe threats to life and property

AMBER alerts
Child abduction emergency bulletins

Test alerts
Receive carrier tests and monthly tests from
the safety alert system

Find and open Settings, then hit Notifications to
customize these notifications. Next, choose Wireless
emergency alerts from the advanced options menu.
Depending on your carrier, you may have access to
several choices, such as:

- Warnings sent out by the federal government on
  a nationwide scale are known as national alerts.
  There is no way to disable these notifications.
- Dangers that are very dangerous, like hurricanes
  or flash floods, may cause significant damage or
  loss of life.

- Extreme danger: Extreme danger to human life and material possessions. Seen as somewhat less hazardous than severe dangers.
- Child abduction emergency bulletins: AMBER warnings.
- Public service announcements: steps to do to prevent harm to people or their property.
- Alerts about testing: The safety alert system notifies of carrier tests and planned tests. What some carriers may refer to as "State and local tests" will apply here.
- View your prior alert history in the event of an emergency.
- Emergency Notifications List for Galaxy Phones

Here are some possible explanations as to why you could not be getting emergency alerts:

- Cell reception is not good on your smartphone.
- You have either disabled emergency notifications or put your smartphone into aero-plane mode.
- While on the phone, certain devices will not display an alert. This differs from one model to another.
- The cell site to which your device is linked is either not sending the alert at the moment, is experiencing maintenance, or is not operational.

If your device keeps getting the same emergency warning, consider turning it off and then back on again.

Modify the setting for app notifications.

You likely use some applications on your phone or tablet regularly, such as those for texting and music. You have the option to read, block, or snooze app alerts according to your preferences. Alternatively, you may customize the vibrations and noises that notify you of critical messages so that you can be notified immediately.

Configure notifications under the Notifications menu.

Enable the history of notifications.

When reading a notice, have you ever closed it by accident? You may see your most recent notifications in their original form using the Notification history function. Notifications of critical events, such as system upgrades, will now always reach you.

1. Find the Settings menu and open it.
2. First, go to Notifications. Then, choose Advanced settings.
3. After that, hit the toggle up top, and then tap Notification history. This is where you will see your notification history going forward.
4. If you haven't seen anything on this page yet, check back later after you've gotten more alerts.

TIPS FOR PERSONALIZING YOUR PHONE'S QUICK SETTINGS PANEL

Galaxy phones have a Quick Settings panel that allows you to access frequently used functions quickly. Determine how to maximize its benefits.

A notification panel, or what Galaxy handsets from Samsung call the Quick Settings panel, is standard on all Android phones. It's a place to manage your phone's fundamental functions including Wi-Fi, Bluetooth, audio, aero plane mode, and more.

This tutorial will teach you how to change the appearance of your Galaxy's Quick Settings panel. In addition, we will suggest which buttons would be most helpful to have on the panel.

The Galaxy Device Quick Settings Panel: How to Access It

Swiping down from the top of the screen or the home screen will bring up the Quick Settings panel, which consists of five buttons in a row. To access the whole page and more buttons, just swipe down; a single page can only have a maximum of twelve buttons.

Five buttons on the Samsung Quick Settings panel

You may quickly access all of a page's buttons by swiping down from the status bar with two fingers. If you want to access a different set of buttons, you may swipe horizontally across pages.

You should probably put the ones you use most often on the top page as some of them could be more helpful to you than others. We'll figure out a way to achieve it.

The Galaxy Device Quick Settings Panel: How to Personalize It

You may personalize the Quick Settings panel by tapping the Add (+) button on the final page. A new set of buttons has been added to the top of the screen; at the moment, they are inactive, but you may always activate them if you think they would be beneficial.

The amount of buttons varies from one device and app to another.

Panel for Samsung's Quick Settings Integrate button types

Buttons for Samsung's Quick Settings

Screen for Samsung's Quick Settings Extra dim

Look around; maybe you'll find a button that piques your curiosity. To bring them back to the main page, long-press on the ones you like. The same method applies to repositioning each button. Select "Done" to commit your changes. If you make a mess, don't fret; just hit Reset to return to the initial setup.

Try These 9 Convenient Settings Buttons!

Now that you understand how to personalize the Quick Settings window, we have some suggestions.

1. Decreased

This function is ideal for those who work best at night. Even when set to 0% brightness, many smartphone users still find their screens excessively bright for nighttime usage. Extra Dim allows you to lower the brightness to a minimum.

You can see it in action with a simple touch, and its intensity can be adjusted with a lengthy push. Here, however, use caution. You may lose all screen visibility if you crank up Extra Dim's intensity and turn down all screen brightness.

Using Extra Dim will not make any screenshots you snap using the feature darker.

2. Dolby Atoms

If you haven't experienced Dolby Atoms on your Samsung smartphone yet, you're losing out. Dolby Atoms is a system that pretends to be surround sound in case you've never heard of it. Feel free to give it a go—just remember to put on your headphones for the full effect.

Fast Settings for Samsung with Dolby Atoms

Customization options for Samsung's Dolby Atoms

To access other modes including Music, Movie, and Voice, just long-press the button. The Auto mode is the default for Dolby Atmos, which means it will identify your current listening environment and modify the sound appropriately. However, changing the mode by hand is simple.

3. Samsung's Children

For parents who want to provide their children with a secure online space where they can play games, do activities that are appropriate for their age, and learn new things without spending a dime, Samsung Kids is an excellent tool to use.

The symbol for Samsung Kids' Quick Settings

64

Games for Samsung Kids

The parental settings for Samsung Kids

Activating the function will cause a complete overhaul of your device's user interface, revealing downloaded games and entertainment. Additionally, you have the option to modify the home screen, see screen time graphs, enable or disable certain rights, and much more.

4. Scanning the QR Code

Quickly navigating the web or completing a purchase are just two examples of the various uses for QR codes. Many stores in your area likely have QR stands set up at the register so customers may pay more quickly.

Samsung included a QR scanner in the Quick Settings menu, which is convenient considering how often we use QR codes. Scan the code with a single press of the button and a camera-pointing motion. To scan QR codes with your Samsung smartphone, you have additional options as well.

There is a QR code scanner on the Samsung quick settings menu.

Scan QR codes using Samsung's camera

Findings from a Samsung QR code scanner

5. Private File

Samsung has developed a Secure Folder to ensure the privacy of its users. It's a private area where you may save sensitive files and information. No one else than you can open the files in this folder since it is password-protected using your biometrics.

Put sensitive media files (pictures, movies, audio recordings, PDFs, etc.) in the Secure Folder and secure it with a password. For those who are interested, guidance on using Samsung Secure Folder is available.

6. Superb Data Conservation.

Built into Samsung phones is a function that lets you limit mobile data use while you're not connected to a Wi-Fi network. On Android, it's called Data Saver mode.

With this feature turned on, your phone will automatically compress data to decrease bandwidth requirements and restrict the amount of data that background applications may utilize. For situations like traveling or when your mobile data (cellular data) is running low, this is a lifesaver for keeping important applications running.

7. Modes

The Quick Settings panel's Modes button is an offshoot of One UI 5's Modes and Routines automation functionality. You may be familiar with Bixby Routines; this is just an improved version of them.

Maybe you're familiar with Samsung's routine creation process. Alternatively, you may use Samsung's modes, which are pre-programmed procedures, to get up and running quickly. One way to access your preferred Mode fast is by using the button located in the Quick Settings window.

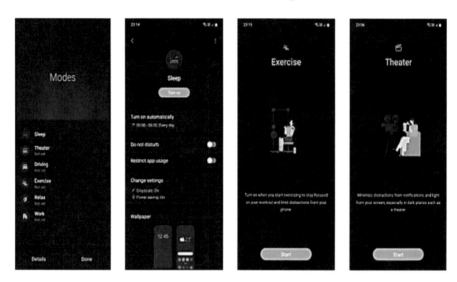

Listed in the Samsung Quick Settings panel are the modes

Samsung Altering the Sleep Mode

Activate Exercise Mode with Samsung

The Samsung Theatre Mode was put up.

Work and Sleep modes are now just called "Modes," replacing the older "Focus" and "Bedtime" options in the Digital Wellbeing menu.

8. Windows Link

If you're not already using the Link to Windows software to link your phone to your Windows PC, you're losing out. On Samsung phones, it is already installed.

After you connect your phone to your computer, you'll have access to a world of features that your phone normally wouldn't have. You can check your messages, make and receive calls, access your picture gallery, adjust your phone's settings, and much more.

9. A Screen Recorder

You may have tried using an unofficial screen recording program in the past if you're a gamer who wants to document their sessions. However, this is much simpler to do with a Samsung smartphone. After finding Samsung Screen Recorder in the Quick Settings panel, all you have to do is touch on it to enable it and then choose the sound settings you want.

An application for recording the screen on Samsung devices

Sound options for the Samsung screen recorder

Screen recording toolbar features on Samsung devices

You won't find these kinds of useful features on other applications, but they're all packed into this one. Getting the most out of Samsung Screen Recorder is easy if you follow our tutorial.

Make the Most of Your Presets

When you need to quickly access frequently used settings or interact with your device, the Quick Settings panel is a lifesaver.

Following the aforementioned steps will allow you to personalize the panel so that you have easy access to the functions you use most often, allowing you to boost your productivity and quality of life.

HOW TO PERSONALIZE YOUR GALAXY PHONE'S KEYPAD

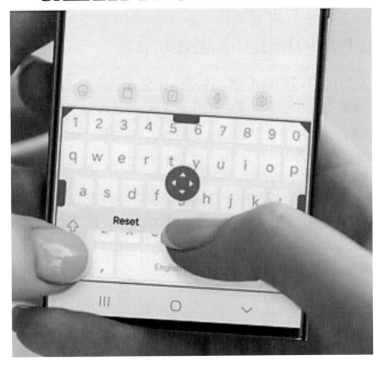

You may customize your phone's keyboard to suit your needs, whether you're looking to send lighthearted messages to pals or write out some serious text. You have the option to send emojis, change the language of the keyboard, alter the default keyboard, and even use your voice to text.

Depending on your wireless carrier, software version, and phone type, the screens and options that are available to you may differ. The standard Samsung Keyboard is the only one that has to be configured in this way.

Modifying the keyboard

The adaptability of the default Samsung Keyboard is one of its best features. Any combination of language, layout, theme, size, feedback, and user-defined symbols is at your fingertips.

Find Samsung Keyboard under parameters, click on it, and then tweak the parameters to your liking. The Settings icon on the keyboard's toolbar also provides access to this page.

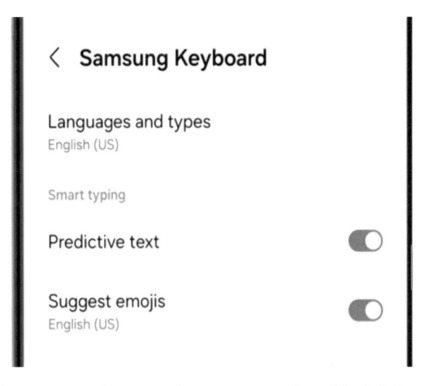

As an example, a new language may be added. Select the language you want to use by tapping on Languages and types, then Manage input languages. To add more languages to your app, just press the download button that appears next to each language.

You may switch to the new language by going to the Samsung Keyboard and tapping the globe-shaped icon for languages. To toggle between languages, tap the symbol once more.

Android Keyboard from Samsung with Settings Icon Shown

Want to alter the appearance of the keyboard? You may personalize your whole gadget using themes.

Make use of the keyboard's toolbar

Funny GIFs and stickers may be sent to friends and family regardless of their phone brand. They will be transformed into a multimedia message on your phone automatically.

Find Messages in your menu, and then choose new chat. Tap the Enter message area to bring up the keyboard after entering or selecting a recipient. The toolbar will show up without your intervention.

You can access the fun features like Emojis, Stickers, GIFs, Voice Input, and Settings from the toolbar. If you want to access even more settings on your phone, tap the Expand toolbar (the three horizontal dots).

Displaying settings and choices above keys, this Samsung keyboard

Disabling the toolbar is an option you have if you are unhappy with it or seldom use it. When the keyboard is active, you may access the settings by tapping the icon in the toolbar. Remove the Keyboard toolbar from your screen by tapping the corresponding button. To activate it again, go to Settings, type in "Samsung Keyboard," choose it, and then touch the switch once again.

Speak as you type

Samsung voice input and Google Voice Typing are the two speech-to-text programs that come preinstalled on your phone. The Samsung Keyboard is the only device that supports Samsung's voice input feature.

1. Find and enter Settings to enable these functions.
2. Select the Keyboard list and default from the General administration menu. Google Voice Typing may be activated by tapping the corresponding switch.

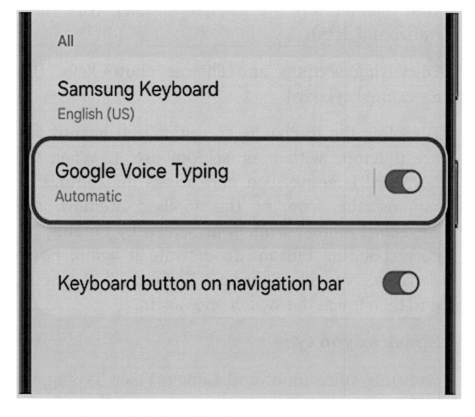

Locate the switch beside the Samsung voice input

3. Pick a voice input method after tapping Samsung Keyboard, then swiping to Voice input. Once you're done, hit [Back].
4. At this point, you may use your voice to dictate a message. Launch the Messages app and start a new discussion.
5. On the toolbar of your keyboard, tap the microphone icon.

Highlighted Voice Input Icon on Samsung Keyboard

6. To have your voice converted into words, just speak into the microphone while it's active.

You could be prompted to agree to terms or grant certain permissions if this is your first experience with Samsung voice input.

Alter the keyboard's layout

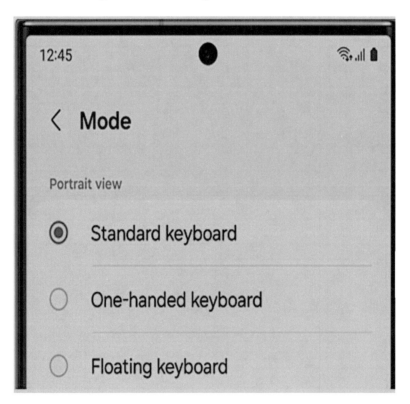

You may still be getting the hang of typing on your Galaxy phone, despite how much you like it.

Fortunately, you can make typing simpler by switching between four distinct keyboard styles.

Press General management when you get to Settings. Go to the Samsung Keyboard's settings and hit the Mode button.

Here are the keyboard modes you have to pick from:

A variety of keyboard modes

- Keyboard standard: When your phone's on-screen keyboard is expanded to cover the full screen, this is the regular keyboard view.
- To enable the one-handed keyboard mode, move the cursor to the screen's right side. To move the keyboard to the left, press the left arrow symbol.
- The keyboard as a floating popup in the screen's center is what you get when you switch to this mode.
- Landscape mode, or using a bigger device as a tablet or Z Fold, causes the keyboard to split in half while using this mode.

Alter the keyboard's default settings

Something spectacular is about to happen as you type. You may get a variety of keyboards to suit your taste in the Play Store and the Galaxy Store.

Go to Settings and then hit General management once you've downloaded a keyboard. Select "Default keyboard" from the keyboard list. Choose your preferred keyboard layout from that menu.

Optional AI and smart typing

With Samsung's smart typing features, like as emoji and text suggestions, the keyboard may be a lifesaver. When you start typing, tools like emoticons and stickers will pop up in the toolbar, allowing you to embellish your messages with ease. Click on General management in Settings, then touch on Samsung Keyboard settings if you need to change these choices. Select the option(s) under "Smart typing" and then press the corresponding switch (es):

Create your shortcuts for often-used phrases in text.

- For those who need help writing, the Galaxy S24's new AI functions may be adjusted here. To toggle Galaxy AI on or off on the keyboard, tap on Chat translation or Style and grammar.
- The predictive text feature allows the keyboard to propose new words to you as you type. Adding the word to your message is as easy as clicking on it.
- The keyboard will provide emoji suggestions based on your current input.
- As you type, the keyboard will propose stickers that it thinks might go well with what you're entering.
- With auto-replace enabled, the keyboard may automatically swap out words as you type. To use the new term, press the Enter key or the space bar.
- Configuration options for the Samsung Keyboard on Galaxy phones
- Make suggestions for textual edits: the keyboard will fix grammatical and phrasal errors automatically. Underlined in green will be suggestions. Selecting which applications will be notified of text errors is also possible by tapping Manage apps.

Extra choices for typing: Go into the options and change things like Auto spacing and Auto capitalization.

Change the keyboard's size

Perhaps a little bigger or smaller keyboard might suit your needs. The good news is that the keyboard can be resized.

1. Choose General management from the menu that appears after opening Settings. From there choose Samsung Keyboard settings.

2. To change the size and transparency, swipe to the options and press on them. Then, use the keyboard's side handles to move the slider to your desired position.
3. To navigate the keyboard, press and hold the middle arrow button. After that, hit the "Done" button.
4. Simply tapping the Reset button will return the keyboard to its default size.

Take away the vocabulary terms that have been learned

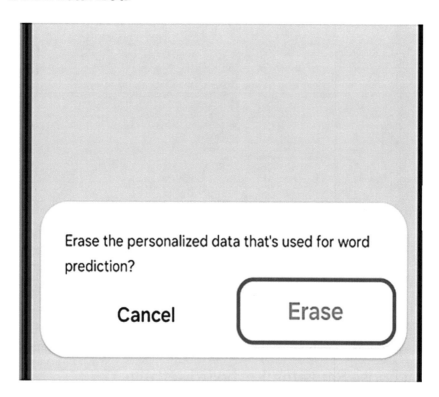

Erase the personalized data that's used for word prediction?

Cancel   Erase

Remove individualized forecasts

In addition to learning new words as you type, the Samsung keyboard will remember the terms you use most. You can erase the words you've learned if you ever need to start afresh.

Swipe down to the bottom of the Settings screen once you find and choose Samsung Keyboard. Before you erase your personalized forecasts, press reset to default settings. Select Delete.

Remove all user input

You may quickly and simply restore the keyboard to its factory settings if you accidentally customize it too much. Swipe down to the bottom of the Settings screen once you find and choose Samsung Keyboard. Choose one of the following options after tapping Reset to default settings:

Reset to default settings

Reset keyboard settings

Erase personalized predictions

Erase personalized touch recognition data

Clear cache Labs

- Turn back the clock to the factory defaults by resetting your keyboard. Downloaded languages will remain intact.
- Get rid of personalized predictions: Get rid of word prediction data. Removing taught words is another benefit of this.
- Data about personalized touch recognition should be deleted.

Select Erase from the menu that appears. If you would want to clear everything, you may do so by selecting all three choices.

CHAPTER FOUR

HOW TO TRANSFER TEXT BETWEEN YOUR PHONE AND GALAXY BOOK LAPTOP

How to Transfer text between your Galaxy phone and Galaxy Book laptop using Nearby Share

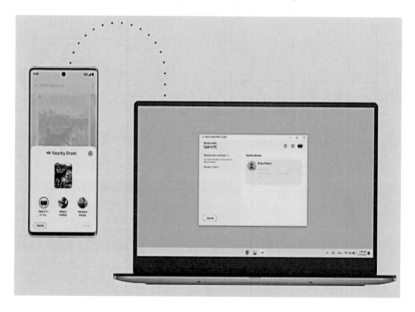

The Nearby Share app for Windows was unveiled by Google at CES 2023. Using the Nearby Share function, users may transfer files between their Android handset and a Windows PC. Nearby Share is among the numerous applications that provide this feature; nevertheless, it is also one of the most dependable, updated for all Android devices, and easiest to use. It has greatly simplified the process of transferring files across Windows and Android devices. But there's another great feature of Nearby Share that not many people know about.

The Nearby Share app makes it easy to transfer text between Android and Windows devices, and vice versa. By storing the text in a note-keeping software on one device and then viewing the same note on the other, users may often transfer text from an Android mobile to a Windows PC, or vice versa. People also use messaging applications like WhatsApp to communicate across the two platforms; they just open the app on their other devices, copy the content from the conversation, and paste it.

All of that trouble is taken care of via Nearby Share. You can easily transfer text from an Android mobile to a Windows PC, or vice versa. In addition to being a piece of cake, the following is how you may transfer content and connections between the two services:

Connecting an Android phone to a Windows computer for texting

1. With an Android device, you may long-press on the text you want to choose. A menu with many

choices has just been shown in the pop-up window.

2. You may use the 'Nearby Share' feature by tapping the 'Share' button.
3. When you choose the Nearby Share option, the user interface will display all the nearby Windows (and Android) devices that are accessible for sharing. Verify that Windows' Nearby Share program is active.
4. To transmit the chosen text to a specific device, choose that option. You may see the text you sent from your Android handset on your Windows PC via a pop-up window.
5. Two choices will appear on your Windows PC if the text you supplied is a link: Copy and Open. If you want to copy the text to your PC's clipboard, use the first option. The second choice will launch your browser and display the URL. The Copy option will be the only one available if the text you supplied does not include a link. To copy the text to your device's clipboard, just click on it.

Transferring Text between a Windows Computer and an Android Device

1. On a Windows PC, you may copy certain text by choosing it and then hitting Ctrl + C at the same time.

2. On a Windows computer, launch the Nearby Share software.
3. On a Windows PC, you may activate the Nearby Share software by clicking on its title bar.
4. On a Windows PC, press Ctrl + V at the same time to paste the copied text into the Nearby Share program.
5. You may see a list of neighboring devices on the right side of the window.
6. And that's all; just choose the Android smartphone you want. A pop-up window will appear on your Android phone, showing you the SMS that you sent from your Windows PC. After that, you'll be able to copy the text or, in the case of links, access them immediately in your device's browser.

Make sure that both devices are linked to the same Wi-Fi network and that their Bluetooth is enabled. Keep in mind that Windows users may only download the Nearby Share app while it's still in beta. Although the software is faultless for the majority of users, there may be a small percentage that has problems. Google has just made the app accessible globally, so you may install it on your Windows PC no matter where you reside, but there is currently no information on when the stable version of the app will be released.

HOW TO SIGN UP FOR A SAMSUNG ACCOUNT

To create an account, go to Samsung's website from any web browser or go to your device's Settings app.

Things to Know

- Click the "Create account" button on the top of the page when you visit account.samsung.com in any web browser.
- Contact number: The process of adding a new account may be found in the following menu: Settings > Accounts and backup > Manage accounts > Add account > Samsung account > Create account.
- You may remotely remove data, lock your phone, and find it using a Samsung account.

Read this article to learn how to sign up for a Samsung account on any Samsung smartphone or in any web browser.

Signing Up for a Samsung Account on a Personal Computer

See below for instructions on how to set up your phone with a Samsung account, but you can also use any online browser to do it later.

1. In any web browser, open the Samsung Account page and click the "Create account" button on the top right.

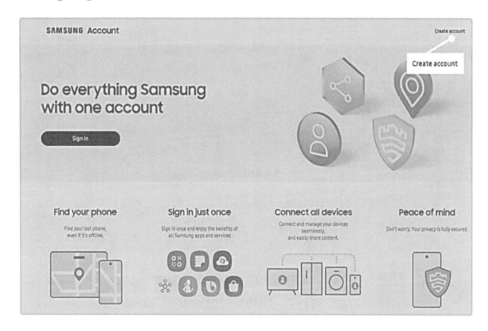

The Samsung Account website prominently displays the opportunity to create an account.

2. By checking the box next to each item and then clicking the Agree button at the bottom, you are indicating your acceptance of the conditions & Conditions, special conditions, and Notice of Financial Incentives.

On the legal agreements page for Samsung Account, the first three circles and Agree are underlined.

3. Pick a password, enter your email address, and fill out your profile details before clicking the Next button to finish the registration process.

The form to create your Samsung account has the Next button selected.

4. You should have received an email from Samsung with a code. Put the code into the designated space on the webpage. Click on the Next button.

On the Samsung Account screen, you can see the highlighted text box and the Next button.

5. Launch your Samsung account by clicking the done button on the last screen.

The Samsung Account On-Device Setup Guide

You may link your Samsung account to your phone using the Settings app's Manage accounts section.

The processes for creating a Samsung account are the same across all devices, even if your phone's UI looks different from the images below.

1. Navigate to Accounts and backup in your phone's Settings app.

You need to delete the existing Samsung account from your phone before you create a new one.

2. Tap To access your accounts.
3. Select the "Add account" button.
4. From your phone, you may access a catalog of all the available accounts. The dot next to an active account will be colored, whereas the dot next to an inactive account will be grey. Go ahead and choose your Samsung account.

   To proceed, you'll need access to a data network or Wi-Fi.

5. When prompted, choose "Create account" from the Samsung account page.

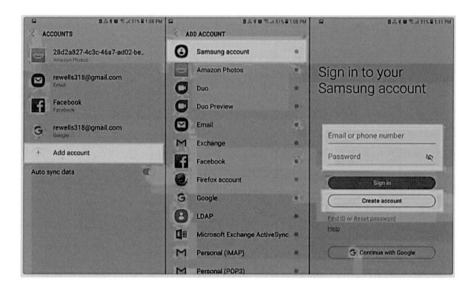

Detailed instructions for signing up for a Samsung account using an Android handset.

Instead, you may use this page to log in using an existing Samsung account, such as the one you registered on your computer.

6. Mark "I have read and agree to all of the above" to indicate your acceptance of the conditions and terms. To proceed, tap Agree.
7. After you've entered your name, email address, and password (among other details), click the "Create account" button.
8. Click OK to register your number if prompted to set up two-factor authentication.
9. For the last step in creating your Samsung account, open your email and click the link that

Samsung provided you. This will allow you to confirm your email address.

Why Create an Account with Samsung?

The creation of user accounts is generally encouraged by smartphone makers and often grants access to additional features and services. If you sign up for a Samsung account, you'll have easy access to some services, and if your phone becomes lost or stolen, you can quickly and easily find it, turn it off, or delete all of its data.

Among other things, you may perform the following with a valid Samsung account:

- Please find your phone.
- Lock and unlock your phone from a distance.
- Put your phone's Samsung Pay, Bixby, Health, or Pass (biometrics) to good use.
- Make sure to save a copy of your data and picture album.

After you sign up for a Samsung account, you can use all of Samsung's services without making any more accounts.

You need to create a Google account to use any Android phone. In contrast, your Samsung account provides access to capabilities unavailable elsewhere.

Account Features for Samsung

Signing up for a Samsung account grants access to a plethora of functions, including those for your phone, TV, computer, and more that are compatible with Samsung products.

Look for My Phone

If you have a Samsung account, this is a must-have feature. If you sign up for Find My Mobile, you can use it to track your lost phone. You may remotely lock your phone, set it to ring (in case you believe it's close but lost), and even choose a number that calls to your lost mobile can be directed to when you track it.

Another option is to remotely erase all data, including sensitive information, from the phone if you do not expect it to be returned to you.

Samsung Locate My Mobile's Route

Cloud by Samsung

Relax if you're the kind of person who shoots a ton of pictures but can't seem to get them saved to your computer. Every so often, Samsung Cloud will automatically back up your files. Prepare your device for syncing:

- Various jobs and upcoming events
- Names, phone numbers, email addresses, and the like
- Images, films, and narratives
- Data about predictive text
- Voice memos, pictures, and tasks
- Important Notices

- Android devices' bookmarks, active tabs, and saved pages Worldwide web
- Samsung Transfer login credentials
- Photographs, scrapbooks, screen captures, and URLs
- Files, favorites, and action notes in S Note

Samsung Medical

When it comes to your health, Samsung Health is your one-stop shop. It can sync with running applications to provide you with all the information you need in one spot, and it also helps you keep track of your workouts and water consumption. The goal of this program, which has a lot of features, is to give you command over your health.

PENUP

If you're an artist who loves to share your work with others, you should check out Samsung's PENUP app. Produce stunning digital artwork with the S Pen and your mobile device.

HOW TO PASSWORD RESET YOUR SAMSUNG ACCOUNTS

Relax if you find yourself gazing at a blank screen on your Samsung Galaxy while you try to retrieve your Samsung account password. The protectors of our digital realm, passwords may easily be forgotten or buried in thought.

This helpful guide will be there for you whether you're in the midst of the excitement of setting up your brand-new Galaxy device or are struggling to remember the extra character you added to your normal password.

Are you trying to improve the security of your Samsung account or have you encountered the dreaded "Forgot my Samsung password" obstacle? Resetting or changing the password for your Samsung account is a breeze with our detailed instructions.

To reset the password for your Samsung account,

Has the memory of your Samsung password slipped your mind? Never fear. To reset the password for your Samsung account, please follow these instructions. If you've forgotten your password and can't get in, follow these steps.

What to do if you've forgotten your Samsung ID?

To restore your Samsung password, you will need your Samsung ID. To recover your ID if you have misplaced it, you must first determine what it is. To do this, just follow these steps:

1. To retrieve your Samsung ID, visit account.samsung.com.
2. Choose "Sign in" and then hit "Find ID."
3. Just type in your recovery number or email address.
4. A verification code should be in your inbox or other communications.
5. On the page for recovering your Samsung ID, enter the code.

The Samsung ID may be retrieved

If you've forgotten your password but still have your Samsung ID, follow these simple steps to reset it. Following the recovery of your lost Samsung ID, you need additionally follow these steps:

1. The email address associated with your Samsung account or Samsung ID must be entered.
2. To change your password, just follow these steps.

Methods for updating the password on your Samsung account

For security reasons, it may be required from time to time to change the password for your Samsung account. I'll show you how to accomplish it.

In the palm of your hand

Here are the procedures to take if you happen to have your Samsung phone on hand:

1. Click on "Settings" and then touch on your name up top.
2. Choose "Privacy and security."
3. Select "Password" and carefully review the conditions.
4. Please choose the "Change" option.
5. Put in both your old and new passwords.
6. To save the changes, use the "Save" button.

Using the web browser

Any device that can connect to the internet can help you change your Samsung password. Here are the steps to fulfill your request:

1. Select "Reset password" from the menu.
2. Simply provide your Samsung ID, which might be your email or phone number.
3. Pick the authentication method (email or mobile phone).
4. You may change your password by following these instructions.

For a Samsung account, what is the minimum password requirement?

Making a strong password is the first step in protecting your Samsung account. Password rules implemented by Samsung are not ordinary impediments. Their purpose is to protect your account from cybercriminals by increasing the difficulty of cracking your password.

Important considerations to bear in mind while creating the password for your Samsung account are:

- At least eight characters.
- Uppercase and lowercase letters combined.
- A minimum of one digit or symbol must be included.

Use WordPress to protect your passwords.

Now that you know how to change or reset your password for your Samsung account, the most important thing is to keep them safe. The handy NordPass password organizer is useful in this situation. Its characteristics provide an unmatched degree of ease and safety.

Utilize NordPass to do the following:

1. Protect sensitive information by storing it in a vault. This includes credit card numbers, personal data, passkeys, and passwords.

2. Autosave makes it easy to save login information and autofill makes it easy to fill out web forms.
3. Keep all of your passwords in sync automatically across all of your devices.
4. This Password Generator will generate strong, one-of-a-kind passwords for you.
5. Find out whether a password is weak, outdated, or overused using Password Health.
6. With Data Breach Scanner, you can discover if a data breach has affected your personal information.
7. Use the File Attachments function to securely save files up to 3GB in size.

In today's digital environment, passwords shouldn't be complicated. Your passwords will be safe, unique, and easily accessible with WordPress. Samsung has made it much easier to reset your password. Make NordPass a part of your digital life security routine now.

Using WordPress, a premium banner service, you may safely save passwords and more online.

HOW TO TRANSFER FILES TO A BRAND NEW SAMSUNG GALAXY PHONE OVER WI-FI

Transferring files to a brand new Samsung Galaxy phone over Wi-Fi, USB-C, or a personal computer

Learn how to get all of your important data back on a brand-new Galaxy phone.

The highly awaited Samsung Galaxy S24 phones are either sitting beautifully on the display of your local smartphone shop or are just around the corner, depending on when you're reading this. Whatever your reason for being here, we've laid out all the necessary procedures for you to transfer your data to a new Samsung Galaxy phone (S24 or elsewhere) in this article.

You can transfer your data to a new Samsung Galaxy phone in three different ways: via Wi-Fi, a USB-C cable, or your computer. However, all three of these methods involve Samsung's own Smart Switch software, which needs Android 4.3 or later on both devices, so keep that in mind before we begin.

We have a dedicated tutorial on how to transfer data from iOS to Android if you're using an iPhone and would want to make the transition. We also have a guide on how to transfer data from Android to iPhone. Nevertheless, we detail the processes for moving data from an old Android phone to a brand-new Samsung Galaxy phone in the sections that follow.

Equipment Needed

- Two smartphones, one of which is Samsung, both powered by Android 4.3 or later
- The Smart Switch app for Samsung
- A reliable wireless network
- An optional USB-C cable

Any computer with Windows 7 or later installed is welcome.

- A few simple steps to move all your info to your brand-new Samsung Galaxy phone
- To accomplish a Wi-Fi data transfer, use the Smart Switch app on both devices and adhere to the on-screen prompts.
- Just plug in the two devices using a USB-C connection, launch the Smart Switch app on both of them and follow the on-screen instructions to transfer data over USB-C.

Download Smart Switch onto your PC, then connect your old device to your PC using a suitable connection to begin data transfer. Transfer all of your previous phone's data to your computer. Then, while setting up your new phone, choose Restore instead of Backup.

Data transmission over Wi-Fi: the ropes

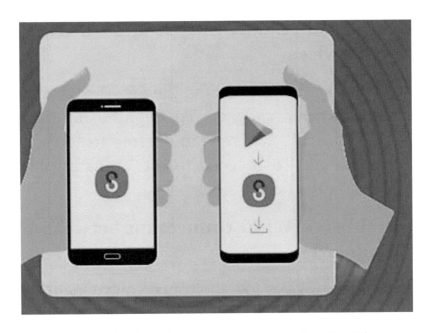

Data transmission from Samsung via Wi-Fi

1. Verify that both devices have Smart Switch turned on.

If you own several Samsung phones, the most convenient method to transfer data like as contacts, images, and music is to use Smart Switch over Wi-Fi. You may locate the Smart Switch app in either the Search or Settings menus on most new Samsung phones. However, Smart Switch may be obtained from the Google Play Store and is necessary for data transfers from devices other than Galaxy ones. A minimum of 1.5 GB of storage space and Android 4.3 or later are prerequisites for this download.

2. Launch the Smart Switch app on each of your devices.

You should start by launching the Smart Switch app on both of your gadgets. To begin using Smart Switch, you must first read and agree to the terms and conditions. To proceed to the Transfer phase, tap Allow on the permissions page.

3. Establish a Wi-Fi connection between the two devices

Join the two devices together once you've made sure they're both linked to the same wireless network. Press Send data, followed by Wireless, on the previous phone. Navigate to Wireless on your brand-new Galaxy phone by tapping on Receive data, followed by Galaxy/Android.

4. Share information across many devices

Choose the quantity of data you want to transfer, then tap Allow on your previous phone. To start the migration, tap Next. The remaining time will be shown graphically as a percentage. Press Return to Home when you're finished.

Steps for Using A Usb-C Cable To Transfer Data

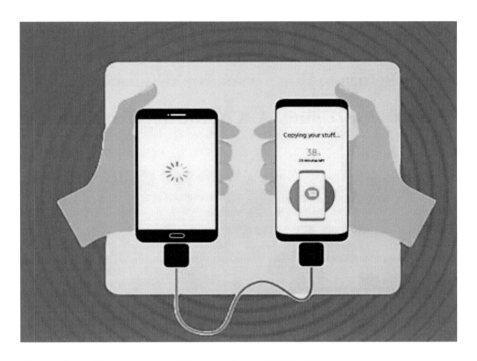

Syncing Samsung files using USB-C

1. Plug in both devices via USB-C.

Just launch the Smart Switch app on both devices and repeat steps 1 and 2 above to transfer data using a USB-C connection. Next, use the USB-C cable that came with your Samsung phone to link the two devices.

2. Share information among various devices

Choose Backup from the Smart Switch app on your brand-new Samsung phone, and then tap Allow. To begin the migration, choose the quantity of data you want to move, and then touch Start. The remaining time will be shown graphically as a percentage. Press Return to Home when you're finished.

Steps For Using A Computer To Transfer Data

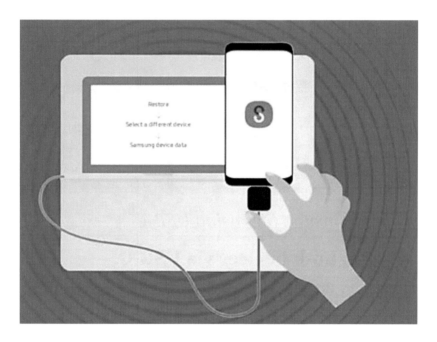

Data transfer from Samsung to PC

1. Get a Smart Switch for your computer.

Before you transfer data using a PC, be sure the PC has Smart Switch installed and that it is running Windows 7 or later.

2. Hook up your outdated gadget to your computer.

After that, use a cable that is compatible with your PC to link your outdated device to it.

3. Transfer all of the information from your previous phone to your computer.

Next, go to the Smart Switch interface on your PC and choose Backup. Then, on your old phone, tap Allow to start the transfer procedure. When you're done, hit OK and then turn off the phone.

4. Link your brand-new gadget to your computer.

The next step is to find a cable that is compatible with your new device and attach it to your computer.

5. Move all of your files to the new gadget.

Pick Restore from the Smart Switch menu on your computer. Tap on Samsung device data, followed by Select a different backup. The data transmission may now commence.

CHAPTER FIVE

HOW TO CREATE A BACKUP OF YOUR SAMSUNG GALAXY DEVICE

One must back up their data before upgrading from an older Samsung Galaxy phone to a newer Galaxy flagship. If you have already saved all of your important contacts, messages, applications, and settings on your old cellphone, migrating to the new one will be a breeze. It is highly recommended that you regularly back up your Samsung phone in case of any issues, unexpected hardware failure, or theft.

Samsung provides many options for backing up your Galaxy phone or tablet in its entirety. There are two options for backing up your data: using the cloud or making a local copy on your computer. Another option for backing up your Galaxy phone is Google Drive. Learn more by following this tutorial.

How does Samsung Cloud work?

The most convenient way to back up your Galaxy phone's data and settings is to use Samsung Cloud, which is available to Samsung account holders. With only a few clicks, you can transfer all of your device settings to a different Galaxy phone.

Contents that may be backed up using Samsung Cloud include as follows:

- Connected Bluetooth gadgets
- Security systems
- Record of phone calls
- Messages
- Settings for the Samsung Keyboard
- Design of the home screen and background
- Permanently Enabled Display Options
- Wi-Fi preferences
- Audio recorder
- Calendar and contact information stored locally in Samsung's applications
- Options for the device, such as an accessibility menu

Samsung Cloud does have a few drawbacks:

- No photographs or documents saved locally will ever be backed up to Samsung Cloud.
- Unfortunately, backups do not include data from non-Samsung applications.
- When moving between Galaxy devices, Samsung Cloud is your only bet. Not many phones are compatible with the cloud service, thus it's not helpful if you don't have a Samsung phone.

Your messages, contacts, and calendar data are backed up by Samsung Cloud, however, it only backs up stuff stored locally. This means that your Google Calendar and Contacts linked with your account will not be backed up.

Even though you probably won't exceed 1 GB of storage space very soon, Samsung Cloud is unable to back up files that are bigger than that. For purposes of privacy and security, all data that is backed up is encrypted.

Data stored in the Samsung Secure Folder is not backed up by Samsung Cloud. If you don't want to lose any data when you reset the device, you need to manually transfer any files from the folder beforehand.

How to use Samsung Cloud to create a backup of your Samsung mobile device

Samsung Cloud's auto backup feature allows you to set your phone to back up once every 24 hours when it's charging, connected to Wi-Fi, and the screen is off.

1. Go into the settings of your Galaxy phone.
2. Click on Accounts and then choose Backup.

3. To access your backup data, go to the Samsung Cloud >> Back up Data.
4. Choose all the things you want to save as a backup.
5. Select "Back up now" to begin the procedure. You have the option to enable auto-resume when traveling if you so want.
6. Hold just a second. Your phone will automatically reboot. After that, tap the Done button at the screen's bottom.

Once you've logged into the Samsung Cloud website, you'll be able to see the backup data stored on your computer.

Methods for retrieving data stored in Samsung Cloud

Samsung Cloud makes it simple to restore a device backup. Unfortunately, Samsung phones are the only ones that support this cloud backup capability. That leaves non-Samsung devices incapable of data restoration.

1. Navigate to the Settings menu on your Galaxy phone.
2. Click on Accounts and then choose Backup.
3. Find the Restore Data option in the Samsung Cloud area.

4. Pick the gadget and the restoration point from which you want to restore.
5. Make sure you want to restore all of your data on your device.
6. To begin, press the Restore button.

Samsung Smart Switch: What Is It?

You may transfer all of your media and contacts from your old device to your new Galaxy phone or tablet with the help of Samsung Smart Switch. You may download the app on your Mac, Windows, or Android device. You may easily transfer all of your data from your old Galaxy phone to your new Samsung phone by using the desktop program to build a complete local backup of your current phone.

Smart Switch, in contrast to Samsung Cloud, backs up anything stored locally on your device. This includes movies, images, and documents. You'll want access to a personal computer, but this backup technique is more thorough than the last one. Here, too, the overall time required for backup and restoration can be greater, contingent upon the volume of data at play.

Smart Switch allows you to do more than just create and restore backups; it also lets you apply firmware updates and return your Galaxy device to its factory settings.

If you're upgrading to a new Samsung phone, you can sync all of your data using the Smart Switch app.

Methods for using Smart Switch for backup purposes on Samsung mobile devices

Using Smart Switch to create a backup of your phone is as follows:

1. Go to Samsung's website and download the Smart Switch app.
2. Start up Smart Switch and then give it the rights it needs.
3. Smart Switch may be downloaded into your Galaxy mobile. Launch the app and enable all of its features.
4. Establish a USB connection between your PC and Galaxy phone or tablet when the Smart Switch applications are active on both devices.

Mac OS X with the Samsung Smart Switch

5. When prompted, tap Allow to provide access to your phone's data.
6. You may back up or restore the linked phone using Smart Switch.

The Mac version of Samsung's Smart Switch program displays the restore and backup options.

7. After you've decided what to back up, click the Backup button. Consider all of your communications, contacts, texts, applications, and system preferences part of this.

8. To start the backup procedure, click on Backup. Keep the Smart Switch app open on your computer or mobile device while you do this.

The Mac version of Samsung's Smart Switch program offers many backup choices.

To continue with the backup, you may need to enable the Keep screen on feature on your Galaxy phone.

Methods for creating an external storage backup of your Samsung device

The capability to immediately back up your Galaxy phone or tablet to an external storage or microSD card is one of the greatest features of the Samsung Smart Switch mobile software. If you want a backup for your phone without delay but do not own a computer or internet connectivity, this is an excellent alternative to consider.

1. Use a USB-C to C connector to attach an external hard drive to your Galaxy device.
2. Go to your Galaxy phone's Settings.
3. Click on Accounts and then choose Backup.
4. Select External storage transfer from the Smart Switch section.
5. To begin backing up your data, choose an appropriate device.
6. Select the files you want to back up, and then hit the Next button.
7. Just follow steps 1–4 again, this time choosing the backup you want to restore from an external storage device under the "Restore from external storage" option.

The Smart Things method for making remote backups of Samsung mobile devices Find

Not only can you start backing up from your phone, but Samsung also gives you the option to do it remotely using a web browser. If your device's screen isn't functioning or you don't have physical access to it, this approach may be a lifesaver when it comes to taking backups.

To set up remote backups for your Galaxy smartphone, you'll need to have an account with Samsung.

You may back up your contacts, calendar events, call history, messages, home screen theme and wallpaper, system preferences, and data from Samsung applications to Samsung Cloud using the remote backup feature.

1. Using a web browser, visit the Smart Things Find website run by Samsung.
2. Use your Samsung Account login information.
3. It will find your phone in a few seconds.
4. Select the device you want to back up from the list on the left side of the screen if your Samsung account is associated with several devices.

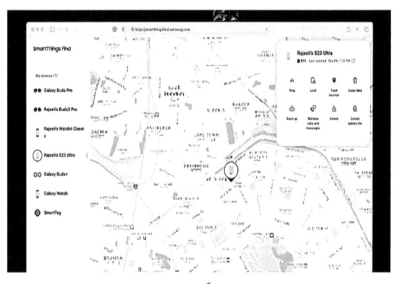

5. Choose "Back up" from the device's status box.
6. After you've decided what information you want to save, hit the "Back up" button.

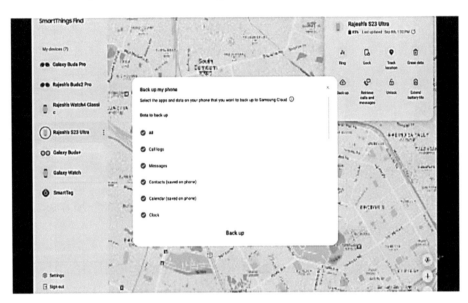

Discover Remote Backup for Samsung Smart Things

7. It can take a few minutes for the backup to finish, depending on how much data there is and how fast the internet is. To dismiss the window after it's finished, click Close.

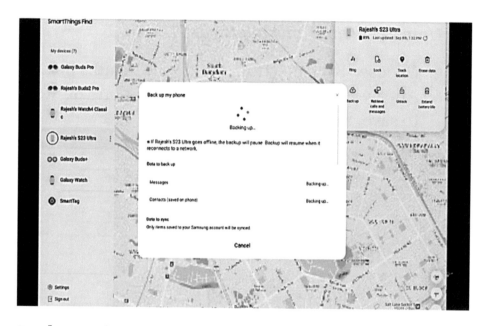

Backup is now underway for Samsung SmartThings.

Even if your Samsung device isn't online at the moment, the backup will start as soon as it is.

Samsung phone backup to Google Drive: the steps

Google Drive is a great alternative to Samsung's account if you'd rather use Google services or don't have one. If the next phone you get isn't from Samsung, you should still follow this procedure.

1. Go to your Galaxy phone's Settings.
2. Click on Accounts and then choose Backup.

3. Select "Back up data" from the Google Drive menu.
4. Select turn on if you have never used Google Drive for backups before.
5. Select "Back up now" to begin the procedure.

Data from some apps, as well as SMS and MMS messages, call logs, and Google account information, are backed up by Google Drive. Think about using Google Photos for your picture and video needs.

During the setup phase of an Android device, you will only have the option to restore a backup from Google Drive. Your data may be restored by resetting it.

Back up your data regularly.

Make backups often, regardless of whether you plan to sell your existing Galaxy phone or not. In this manner, regardless of what happens to your phone, you will never lose any of your data. Plus, Samsung simplifies things by providing many options for backing up your data. All of the aforementioned methods do not back up data from third-party applications, so if you want to restore all of your Android apps at once after a factory reset, you may want to look into Shizuku. You may easily upgrade to a top folding phone with a backup.

HOW TO CONFIGURE SAMSUNG'S FACE RECOGNITION SYSTEM

The Function of Samsung's Face Recognition Technology

Facial recognition's potential applications are well-known. Here, however, is a quick rundown in case you're completely unfamiliar with the subject. One kind of technology that helps with identification verification is face recognition, which uses a person's unique facial traits to do the job. Introduced and extensively used in Samsung phones, it improves security and allows for rapid unlocking. The front-facing camera on your phone captures all of his or her facial characteristics when you hold it. Access is granted as soon as the device's Depth Vision camera verifies your identification.

Configuring and Utilizing Samsung's Face Recognition Technology

Customers loved the facial recognition function on Samsung just as much as the rest of the company's offerings. But, setting up and using facial recognition on Samsung might be confusing for some. Fortunately, you can rely on us. To activate facial recognition on your Samsung S20, S21, or S22, just follow these instructions.

1. Launch your phone's Settings app.
2. Go to Biometrics and security further down the page. After that, choose Face recognition by tapping on it.
   - To set up a secure screen lock (pattern, PIN, or password, for example) if you haven't done so before, touch Continue and then choose one of the available options.
   - You may be prompted to provide your present PIN, password, or pattern to access the security features that you have previously activated.

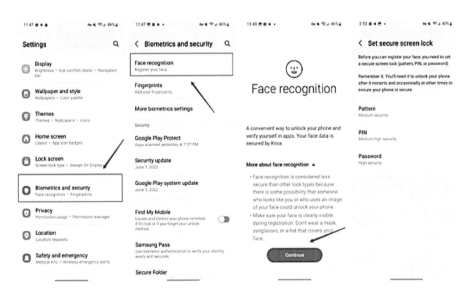

3. Configure face recognition on Samsung S20, S21, and S22 devices.
4. When you're done, keep your Samsung phone around 10–20 inches from your face. Position your face so that it fits within the circle that appears on your phone's screen.
5. Just keep staring at the progress meter until it reaches 100% and follow the on-screen directions.

When the scan is finished, click the "Done" button. The "Face recognition" section gives you more options to tweak the settings to your liking.

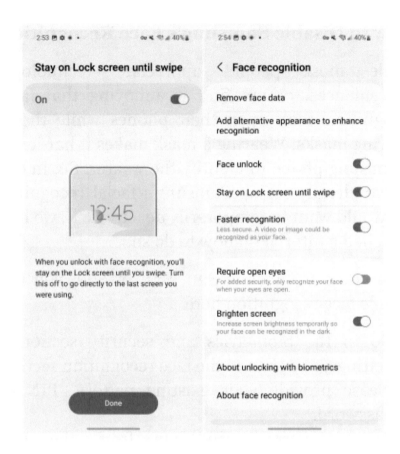

Customize the settings for facial recognition on Samsung

After you finish configuring Samsung Face Recognition, you may unlock your phone just by gazing at it. But there are certain situations when your phone's facial recognition won't work. If you turn off your gadget for a day or restart it, for instance. You won't need anything else.

How to Disable Samsung's Face Recognition

While most people appreciate technology's conveniences, others find it annoying that facial recognition can't open their phones while they're wearing masks. Wearing a mask makes it harder for a Samsung phone to identify the wearer. So, in case you've already set up Samsung's facial recognition but would want to temporarily deactivate it, we have compiled a tutorial on how to do so.

If you own a Samsung S20, S21, or S22, you may disable face recognition here.

1. Go to the biometrics and security section of Settings, and then to the face recognition section.
2. Please provide your existing pattern, PIN, or password.
3. Select Remove face data from the Face recognition options.
4. Choose Remove from the pop-up menu to confirm.

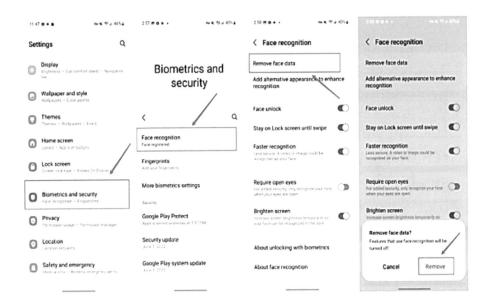

Eliminate the facial recognition feature

It's done! Your Samsung's facial recognition feature has been disabled.

You may toggle the feature next to Face unlock to Off if you just want to deactivate it. Once that happens, using your face to unlock your phone will no longer be an option.

How to Disabling Samsung's Face Recognition When Ensconced

All is OK with Samsung's facial recognition. However, Samsung facial recognition isn't always reliable. Hacks exist to repair the Samsung pass facial recognition not working issue, which might be useful if you have issues with Samsung face recognition and are unable to access your phone. Tenor share 4uKey for Android is the best professional program you can get.

It's an effective and dependable solution for removing the Android lock screen. It only takes a small bit of work to unlock a locked gadget, therefore there's no need to follow complicated processes. Here are the methods to uninstall Samsung's face recognition when locked if you ever find yourself locked out of your phone because of an issue with Samsung's facial recognition.

HOW TO MAKE USE OF YOUR GALAXY DEVICE'S FINGERPRINT SENSOR

A picture of a fingerprint in blue

Your fingerprint is unique among all humans, and no two people are precisely like you. For that reason, Galaxy devices' fingerprint security is rock solid. The specifics of how you use the fingerprint scanner, meanwhile, could vary somewhat from one device type to another.

You'll need an Android 9.0 or later handset to complete these steps. Different wireless service providers, software versions, and device models may have different available screens and options.

Locate the device that can scan your fingerprint.

You may not find the fingerprint scanner in the same spot on all Galaxy phones or tablets. You should be aware of the place before you begin to register your prints.

Phones that have a fingerprint scanner built into the screen:

- The S24, S24+, and S24 Ultra models include
- The S23 Ultra, S23+, S23, and S23 Feel:
- A22, A22+, and an Ultra S22
- 5G S21, 5G S21+, and Ultra 5G S21
- The 5G-enabled S20, S20+, S20 Ultra, and S20 FE
- The S10, S10+, and S10 5G models
- The Note20 Ultra 5G and the Note20 5G
- Ten, Ten Plus, and Ten Plus 5G
- Collections A50–A51–A53–A71–A42–and A52–5G
- Cell phones that can scan your fingerprint from the rear:
- The numbers A11, A20, and A21

- S9, S9+, S8, and S8+
- The Nokia 8 and Nokia 9
- Devices that track fingerprints directly from the screen:
- Slide S5e
- S6 and S6 light tabs
- The S7+ and the S7 FE tabs
- S8+ and Ultra Tabs
- Devices in the S9, S9+, and S9 Ultra lineup

The fingerprint scanner may also be found in:

- Scanners for the Z Fold and Z Fold2 may be found under the Side button. The scanner on the Z Fold5, Z Fold4, and Z Fold3 is located on the side button.
- The side button is where you'll find the scanners on the Z Flip, Z Flip 5G, Z Flip3, Z Flip4, and Z Flip 5.
- The scanner is located on the Power key of the S10e and XCover6 Pro.
- On the side button, you can find the fingerprint scanners for the A54 5G, A25 5G, A23 5G, A32, A15 5G, A13 5G, A13, A12, and A03s.
- A fingerprint scanner can be found on the side button of the Galaxy Tab S7, Tab S8, Tab S9 FE, and Tab S9+ FE.

- Smartphones that record fingerprints when you press the Home key:
- Our S7 and S7 edge models
- S6 and its margin
- Fingerprint scanners integrated into tablet Home keys:
- S3 and Tab S2

Configure and utilize fingerprint unlock

The moment has come to register your prints and enable fingerprint security. Whatever gadget you have, the instructions are almost the same. One key distinction will be the placement of the fingerprint sensor.

1. To access biometrics, go to Settings > Security and privacy > Biometrics. Press on Fingerprints.
2. Punch in the credentials for your lock screen. At this stage, you could be asked to set up a screen lock if you haven't already. Read the information and then click Continue when you're ready.
3. To register your fingerprint, follow the on-screen instructions. To avoid fingerprint registration errors caused by excessive light, cover the fingerprint sensor completely with your finger. Press the Done button when you're done.

4. The next step is to activate the feature that uses your fingerprint as an unlock method.

   If your fingerprint sensor is on the side key or below it, you can stop accidental unlocks by disabling the "Fingerprint always on" option.

5. Pressing the Power or Side key, or tapping the screen, will allow you to unlock your smartphone with your finger. Finding the fingerprint scanner is the next step. Just put the registered finger on it. Once it detects your fingerprint, the gadget will unlock itself.

Take a look at the security settings and choices once you've registered your fingerprint data:

- To change the name of a fingerprint, just touch on it, type in the new name, and then hit the Save button.
- Delete fingerprint information: Select the fingerprint you want to remove, and then press on it.
- You may add up to four fingerprints in total.
- Verify more fingerprints: Verify the identification of the fingerprints that you have recorded.
- Your smartphone can be unlocked with the touch of a fingerprint.

- Even when the screen is turned off, you may still scan your fingerprint.
- Display symbol even when the screen is off: You get to decide when the fingerprint symbol shows up on your screen. Just tap to show, Never, or Always On Display are your options.
- Display an animation to unlock: When you scan your fingerprint, an animation to unlock will be shown.
- Learn how to unlock your smartphone with the use of fingerprints.

Your PIN, password, or pattern, not your fingerprint, will be required after a device restart or after 24 hours of inactivity.

An in-screen sensor may be compatible with the plastic screen protector that comes pre-installed on certain smartphones. Changing the screen protector might impact the ability to recognize fingerprints. Please refer to our troubleshooting guide if you have issues with fingerprint identification.

Provide more fingerprints.

Enhance a Galaxy phone's fingerprint scanning capabilities

Switching up the way you hold your phone or turning it upside down could make using a different fingerprint to unlock it seem more natural. You can add numerous fingerprints, which is great since it means you can unlock your smartphone no matter how you hold it.

1. Select Biometrics from the Security and privacy menu under Settings. Press on Fingerprints.

2. Select "Add fingerprint" after entering your credentials for the secure screen lock.
3. To add the fingerprint, follow the on-screen instructions and then hit Done.

Deactivate your device's fingerprint sensor

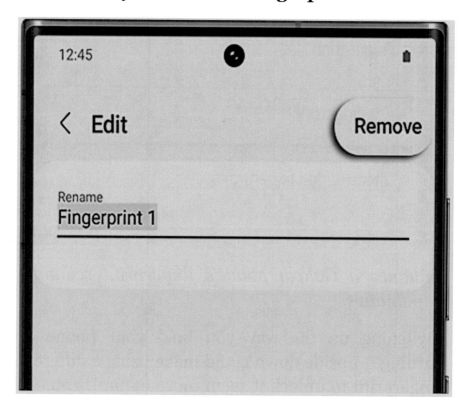

All smartphones running Android 9.0 or later have identical methods for erasing a fingerprint, regardless of where the fingerprint sensors are located.

1. Select Biometrics from the Security and privacy menu under Settings. Press on Fingerprints.
2. After that, input your login information and then choose the fingerprint (e.g., Fingerprint 1) that you want to remove.
3. To confirm, press Remove again after tapping Remove.

In a Galaxy phone, deselect the checkbox that says "Fingerprint."

By default, the Fingerprint unlock function will be disabled if all registered fingerprints are removed.

Having problems using fingerprint to unlock the smartphone

If you want your fingerprint sensor to always function, follow these steps:

- Cover the whole sensor with your finger and keep your grip on the smartphone as you did while configuring the fingerprints.
- Before you start scanning, wipe off your fingers and the scanner.
- If the fingerprint scanner is still not working after restarting the device, try another one.
- Stay current with the device and applications.
- Reapply the fingerprints after removing them.

- Try typing your usual PIN, password, or pattern if you're still unable to unlock your smartphone using the fingerprint sensor.

HOW TO SET UP AND USE SAMSUNG PAY

The steps to activate Samsung Pay

Samsung Pay may be activated using the Samsung Wallet app.

Items that will be required are:

- A gadget that works with Samsung Use the Samsung Wallet app to pay using your nationwide credit or debit card.

Installed pre-installed on certain Samsung smartphones is the Samsung Wallet app. If it isn't already on your device, you can download it here:

1. Both on Google Play and the Galaxy Store.
2. Instructions for assembly
3. Launch the app for Samsung Wallet.
4. Proceed with the setup procedure.
5. Remember to include your Nationwide credit or debit cards.

Keep in mind that you have the option to include:

Using the same card on many devices.

When you shop at stores that have the contactless or Samsung Pay emblem, you can utilize Samsung Pay.

You may pay as much as you like in a single transaction. However, personal restrictions on Samsung Pay purchases may be imposed by individual stores.

Having trouble with Samsung Pay?

If you have problems while attempting to use Samsung Pay, here's what you need to know.

For those who have never used Samsung Pay before

- Verify that your device is current by looking in the settings for any necessary upgrades.
- Verify that your card appears in the Samsung Wallet app. You may be required to complete a few further steps to complete the setup.
- If you're familiar with Samsung Pay,
- Verify whether the store takes Samsung Pay.
- Samsung Pay or other contactless logos should be kept in mind.
- Verify that the card is not in a frozen state.

You may still use Samsung Pay even if you have frozen your debit card because it was misplaced.

The Banking app has many uses:

- Once you've located your card, defrost it. Then, report it as lost or stolen. If your card is misplaced.
- Recovering a Stolen or Lost Credit Card: What to Do
- If you happen to lose or have your card stolen, please inform us without delay.
- You should notify the appropriate authorities if your card is missing or stolen.

If you have misplaced or stolen your card, you may notify us by phone or our banking app. We will revise your order and send you a replacement. Canceling your card prevents you from making any purchases with it. However, Samsung Pay will keep functioning. The gaming restriction will remain in effect even if you turned it off before you reported your card. Samsung Pay will still not be able to be used to pay for gambling.

Your Samsung Pay information will be instantly updated once your replacement card is available.

Stop the use of a lost debit card

Our Banking app allows you to freeze your debit card if you lose it. Once frozen, your card cannot be used to make purchases online or in stores. However, Samsung Pay will keep functioning. Your card may be unfrozen when you've located it.

You may still use our Banking app to toggle the gambling restriction on and off, even while your card is frozen. Payments made with Samsung Pay for gambling will not be processed while the gambling ban is enabled.

CHAPTER SIX

HOW TO UNLINK A SAMSUNG PAY CARD

If you no longer want to use your card, you have the option to delete it from the Samsung Wallet app.

Take out your card

Your device's instructions will tell you how to delete a card from the app.

Please Explain Samsung Pay.

You may use Samsung's mobile payment system to purchase both online and at physical stores.

Mobile payment software and digital wallet service Samsung Pay is developed and maintained by Samsung. Customers may have their loyalty cards and some payment options close to hand, even when they're not using their credit or cash. You may use it in-store, in the app, or on the web. Pay with a simple touch after loading your cards into your devices. You can see the Samsung Pay interface below.

Developed specifically for use with Samsung phones, Samsung Pay is an alternative to Apple Pay and Google Wallet. If you'd rather not utilize Samsung Pay, you have the option to deactivate it.

Retail customers making a transaction using Samsung Pay.

Which Advantages Does Using Your Phone for Payments Offer?

The two primary justifications are ease of use and safety.

You may put your worries about misplacing your wallet to rest when you use mobile payment software such as Samsung Pay. No one else can access your payment methods, even if you lose or leave your device unattended, since the system needs at least one security mechanism, such as a PIN or biometric scan.

For extra peace of mind, you may remotely erase all data from the Samsung Pay app if you activate Smart Things Find and then misplace your device.

First Steps

There is an initial setup process that must be completed before you can use Samsung Pay.

Be sure to check the Samsung Pay compatibility of your smartphone first. It comes preinstalled on a plethora of devices, such as wearables, the Galaxy Z and Note series, and more. The Samsung Pay Supported Devices list has the whole list.

To use Samsung Pay on a Samsung smartphone, you'll need to sign up for a Samsung account, set up a security PIN or fingerprint, and then use a card that is compatible with the service.

The Samsung Pay system also includes Samsung Pay Cash. You may load money onto your digital debit card using Samsung Pay by linking it to your bank account or another app-based credit or debit card.

Using Samsung Pay

Using Samsung Pay is a breeze after you're all set up and have entered your payment options.

Simply place your phone's rear towards the store's contactless scanner and follow the on-screen instructions to finish your transaction. Use the fingerprint scanner, input a PIN, or scan your iris, depending on the security settings you have configured, to unlock your phone.

HOW TO USE SAMSUNG PAY TO KEEP TRACK OF YOUR FAVORITE CARDS

Presenting a phone to a near-field communication reader

Using Samsung Pay's Favorite Cards helps expedite purchases. Even when your screen is turned off, you'll still have access to your cards via the Lock or Home screens. So, you won't have to hold up the checkout queue by emptying your pockets.

Edit the Favorite Cards list

Samsung Pay shows two cards as Favorites.

All of your saved debit and credit cards will automatically be added as Favorite Cards. However, you are free to alter your card selection whenever you want.

Navigate to the Menu on your mobile device to access Samsung Pay. Proceed to Manage Favorite Cards by tapping Settings. Choose which cards to become your Favorite Cards and which ones to remove. Just hit the Back arrow when you're done.

Up to fifteen cards may be designated as your preferred cards.

Get to your preferred cards fast

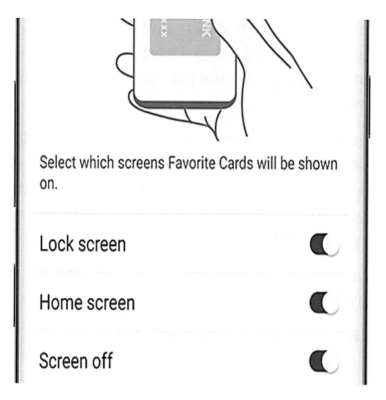

Select which screens Favorite Cards will be shown on.

Lock screen

Home screen

Screen off

Your cards will be instantly accessible after you enable your phone's Favorite Cards function.

Access your Favorite Cards with a simple swipe from the bottom of the screen. They are accessible even when the screen is turned off, on the Home screen, or the Lock screen.

Launch Samsung Pay and then hit Menu to personalize the various Favorite Card locations. Navigate to Quick Access by tapping Settings. You may toggle Favorite Cards on and off for individual screens by tapping the corresponding button.

Pick which cards to display on the lock screen, the home screen, and even while the device is turned off.

Alter the Rank of Preferred Cards

The Favorite Cards section also allows you to reorder your favorite cards for further convenience.

Up from the screen's base, you may swipe to access Favorite Cards. Simply touch and hold a card to move it to where you want it. As soon as the deal is made, the cards will switch places.

When you go to Favorite Cards, the most recent card you used will be there, no matter what sequence the cards are in.

HOW TO DISABLE SAMSUNG PAY

You may do it in two ways: Delete the app or remove your cards.

- Shuffle your deck: Launch Samsung Pay. Navigate to Menu > Cards. Then, choose a card. Finally, see More Options. Card removed.
- Get rid of the software: For Samsung Pay, go to Settings > Apps. Click on Remove. To confirm removing the app, click OK.
- You will lose access to all of your cards, including membership cards when you uninstall the Samsung Pay app.

If you want to deactivate Samsung Pay, you may either delete all of your saved credit and debit cards or uninstall the app. Both of these options are detailed in this post.

Unlinking Your Samsung Pay Account from Your Credit or Debit Cards

Removing linked credit or debit cards is one method to disable Samsung Pay. Staying on your phone is great, but if you don't have any acceptable cards, Samsung Pay won't operate properly. If you find that you require the service at a later time, you may easily rejoin your cards.

1. Select Menu from the three-stripe symbol located in the app's top left corner.

   After starting up Samsung Pay, in some versions, you may access your cards by tapping the symbol on the main screen.

2. Press the Cards.

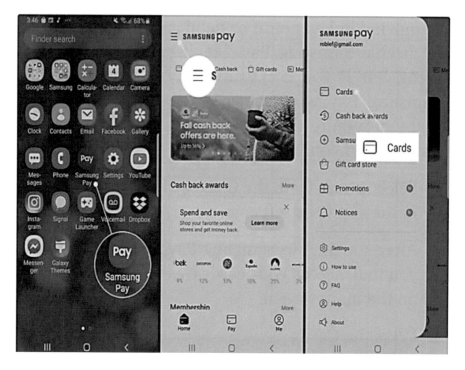

Samsung Pay logo, Menu with three lines, The option for cards

3. Tap More Options after selecting a card.
4. Call up the "Delete card" option.
5. Choose Delete from the confirmation pop-up.

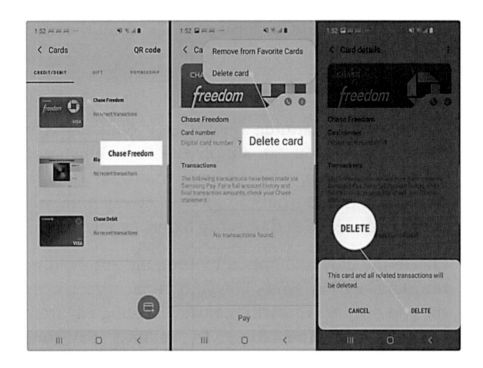

Remove the card The ability to remove confirmation and the card button from Samsung Pay

When you delete a card, Samsung Pay will also erase all of your transaction history.

6. Keep on until you've erased every single payment detail from Samsung Pay.

Even if you delete your cards from Samsung Pay, they will still work in any other app or service. Your debit and credit cards will continue to function independently of the app, in other words. Get in touch with the card issuer if you want to fully cancel your cards.

Steps to Remove Samsung Pay

If you're not planning on utilizing Samsung Pay anytime soon, you can simply delete it. When you uninstall the app, all of your financial data is likewise removed from the service. At any time, you may re-download and re-setup Samsung Pay.

Locate the uninstall option by pressing and holding the Samsung Pay symbol on your Home screen or in the app drawer. This will remove Samsung Pay from your device. The steps to remove Samsung applications from your device's Settings are detailed below.

By doing this, you will also remove any rewards or membership cards from your device. Having said that, this will not remove your Samsung account.

1. For Samsung Pay, go to Settings > Apps.
2. Click on Remove.

This software cannot be deleted from all Samsung smartphones. You may try disabling the program instead of uninstalling it. Just pick Disable instead of Uninstall on this page.

3. Select OK from the confirmation pop-up.

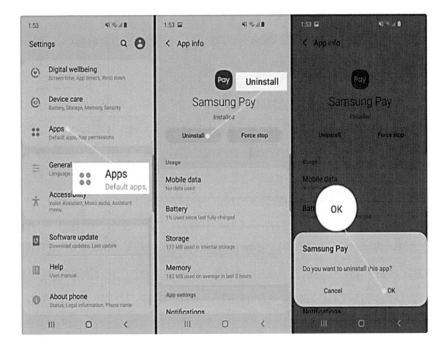

Samsung applications, the Uninstall button, and the OK button

Other Options for Samsung Pay

The fact that many Samsung smartphones come with Samsung Pay makes it convenient. Nonetheless, there are other options for mobile payment apps. There are other alternatives to Apple Pay that Samsung smartphones may utilize, such as PayPal, Cash App, and Google Pay.

HOW TO INSTALL APPS FOR SAMSUNG GALAXY PHONES

If you possess a Samsung smartphone, how do you install apps?

The standard procedure for downloading applications on a Samsung phone is as follows: first, search for the desired program by name; second, choose the app category; third, tap Install; and last, tap Accept and Download. Without further ado, the program will begin downloading and installing itself. After the program has finished downloading, you can find it under the All Applications menu. Anyone attempting to install an app from Samsung will most likely utilize this technique. Everything is taken care of for you, and it's fast and easy. But this approach isn't foolproof every time it comes to sensitive information. Transferring data from a PC to a mobile device could be a bit of a pain and take a while since it doesn't have a backup feature. The good news is that there is a tool available to assist you with this.

Can you tell me about Cool muster Android Assistant, the top app downloader for Samsung devices?

You can't go wrong with the Cool muster Android Assistant. It is packed with features that will streamline and improve your mobile experience. Finding a Samsung applications downloader that works for you and makes transferring files easy is vital since current mobile devices aren't only for making calls; they're also for entertainment and support. Samsung Galaxy customers now have the opportunity to install applications in seconds with the help of the Cool muster Android assistant. With a single click, you may transmit media files like photos, videos, audio, and text. This makes it easy to transfer and update data stored on mobile devices, such as playlists and contact books.

Additionally, this utility can send group text messages, recover backed-up data, and greatly simplify software installation and downloads. Even better, all you have to do to utilize it is follow the two steps I've laid down for you below. Keep in mind that there is a Mac version that can do all the same things on a Mac machine. Get the Samsung Apps Downloader for PC out of the way first. In this case, we'll use Windows as an example.

Methods for Installing Samsung Apps on Galaxy

1. Launch Cool muster and link your PC with your Samsung Galaxy S4.

   Following the download and installation of the Cool muster Android Assistant on your computer, launch the program. Once launched, go to the beginning window and follow the prompts to connect your phone to a computer.

   To make the program identify your Samsung phone, you may have to activate USB debugging on your phone. It may be skipped if it has already been set.

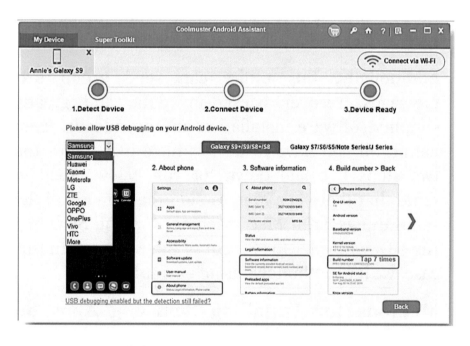

Turn on USB debugging by following these steps:

166

- Go to "Settings" \ Click "Applications" < Click "Development" < Select "USB debugging" if you're using Android 2.3 or an older version.
- To enable USB debugging on Android versions 3.0 to 4.1, go to "Settings," choose "Developer options," and then check the box.
- If you're using Android 4.2 or a later version: Go to "Settings" < Click "About Phone" < Press "Build number" many times until you get a message saying "You are under developer mode" < Return to "Settings" < Click "Developer options" < Select "USB debugging".

To provide the program super user authority, when prompted by an app while USB debugging is enabled, tap "Allow" on your phone.

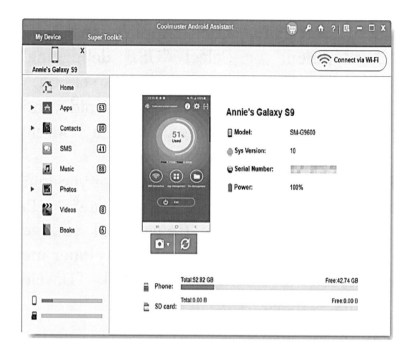

2. Get applications for your Samsung Galaxy S23.

As soon as the Cool muster Android Assistant detects and identifies the Samsung Galaxy S23, a separate window will display all of the data currently stored on the device, including media files, contacts, and more. To access the window where you may manage your apps, click the APPS button.

Click the INSTALL button when you locate the toolbar. Now you can choose from all the available applications, tap the ones you wish to install, and the process should be quick and easy.

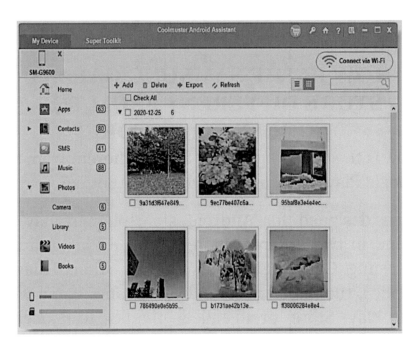

You may remove unwanted programs from your Samsung Galaxy S4 by pressing the UNINSTALL button, and you can transfer apps to your computer by using the EXPORT button.

CHAPTER SEVEN

HOW IS THE SAMSUNG GALAXY STORE DIFFERENT FROM THE GOOGLE PLAY STORE

How is the Samsung Galaxy Store Different from the Google Play Store, and Which One Is Better?

Apps designed for Android smartphones may be found in two different stores: Google Play and the Samsung Galaxy Store. Except for some Huawei phones, the majority of Android phones come with the Play Store preinstalled, thanks to Google's ownership of the app. Only devices manufactured by Samsung may access the Galaxy Store.

You should probably choose one of the two shops to use as your primary app store, as Samsung smartphones come with both. With that being said, which of the two app stores is better for Samsung Galaxy devices, and how are they different from one another?

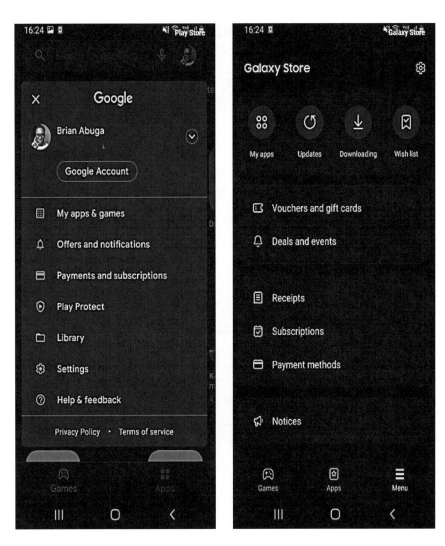

Google Play Marketplace Night mode menuApp Store

The dark mode option of the Samsung Galaxy StoreOnline Shop for Galaxy Products

With their matching rounded app and game icons, both shops look fantastic. You can easily find your favorite game or software on the homepage of both the Play Store and the Galaxy Store by using the search box.

On both stores, you'll see a list of suggested applications immediately below the search box, and further down the page, you'll see suggestions organized by category.

Two tabs, one for applications and the other for games are conveniently located on the homepage. You can access your profile image, the Play Store menu, updates, subscriptions, and settings by tapping on it. By pressing the Menu button, you may reach the same on the Galaxy Store.

Characteristics and Operation

Apps for watch face on the Google Play Store, Samsung Galaxy Store fronts, and AODsOnline Shop for Galaxy Products

When it comes to the fundamentals, both the Play Store and the Galaxy Store are quite similar. Browse, download, and update applications automatically or manually with their help. You may also control the applications that are already available on both platforms. Both shops also include in-app purchases, the ability to manage app subscriptions, and a selection of special offers.

When comparing the two shops, the only real difference is in the extra features each provides.

You may browse your library of films and books that you bought via Google Play on the Play Store. You may access these services via specialized Android applications, but on a PC, you can see them all in one convenient location. Your WearOS watch also can install watch faces from the Play Store.

Extras like Samsung Galaxy device-specific themes and other design components are available at the Galaxy Store. Icons, A.I. displays, stickers, typefaces, and augmented reality designs are all part of this. There are a plethora of free and premium themes to peruse in the Galaxy Store if you're looking for an alternative to Samsung's One UI.

Availability of Apps and Games

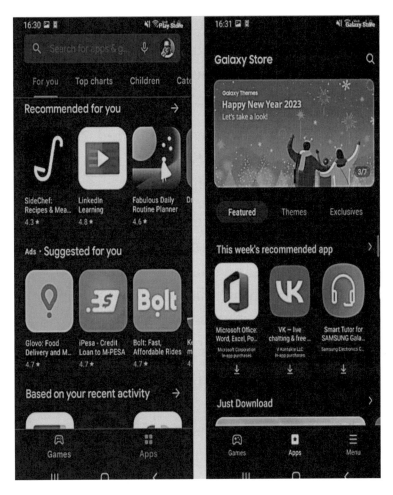

Launch page of the Google Play Store including app tilesApp Store

Listing of apps on the Samsung Galaxy Store homepage online Shop for Galaxy Products

A greater variety of applications are available in the Play Store compared to the Galaxy Store since it is accessible on a much larger number of devices. As of right now, over 3.5 million applications can be found on the Play Store, according to Statista.

To better suit Samsung Galaxy phones and tablets, the Galaxy Store provides a selected collection of applications. The Galaxy Store is the only place you can get some of these applications.

The Play Store has more games than the Galaxy Store, just as the Play Store has more applications. Having said that, the Galaxy Store does provide some unique content, like as the popular game Fortnight. It makes sense to look for new games on the Play Store if you like trying them out.

Before installing a game, make sure it's available on the Galaxy Store. Due to optimization for Samsung Galaxy smartphones, this version is expected to have somewhat improved performance.

Buying Things through Apps

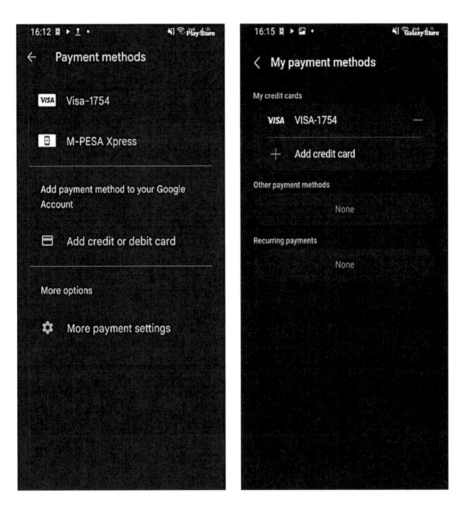

Paying for Google Play: Multiple OptionsApp Store

Store for Samsung Galaxy Devices Various methods of payment online Shop for Galaxy Products

Use the payment methods associated with your Google Account to purchase applications from the

Play Store. Google Wallet, phone billing, PayPal, and other payment methods may be available.

Samsung Pay, major credit cards, debit cards, and phone bills are all accepted at the Galaxy Store. When you initially go to add a payment method and buy an app, you'll need to log in using your Google or Samsung account in the respective stores.

Accounts, Security, and Updates

Whenever an updated version is available in the Play Store, it will silently update itself. After touching your profile image, go to Settings > About > Update Play Store to see if there are any changes. When you open the Galaxy Store, even with automatic updates turned off, it will urge you to update.

A Google account is required to access the Play Store. Since you most likely already have a Google account associated with your mobile device, the Play Store will utilize this one. To access the Galaxy Store on your new Samsung Galaxy smartphone, the first step is to establish a Samsung account.

When it comes to downloading applications and games, both marketplaces provide enough safety. With the addition of Play Protect, the Play Store seems to have a little advantage over the Galaxy Store. You may want to think about installing third-party antivirus software on your smartphone just in case.

App Interoperability All via Google Play and Samsung's app stores

While you may find certain programs in both shops, updating apps requires installing them from the Galaxy Store.

If you want to update an app like Discord that you downloaded from the Play Store, you can't do so automatically or manually via the Galaxy Store. Reinstalling the software from the Galaxy Store will work, but first, you have to remove it from the Play Store.

However, the Play Store works flawlessly with app updates from the Galaxy Store.

Are the Play Store and the Galaxy Store Uninstall able?

Without rooting your phone, you will not be able to remove the Play Store or the Galaxy Store. Your smartphone will be left open to harmful applications and unable to update current apps securely if you deactivate the Play Store, the only option you have.

The Galaxy Store is an integral aspect of Samsung's One UI user interface and must be running continuously regardless of your preferences.

Which Samsung App Store Is Best for You?

The collection of applications offered by the Play Store and the fact that the Galaxy Store is solely designed for Samsung smartphones are the key differences between the two. Except for being able to update the built-in Samsung exclusive applications that are optimized for the One UI skin, using the Play Store wouldn't be missing anything.

Skip the Play Store and you'll lose out on a ton of applications and games, but skip the Galaxy Store and you'll still be able to get by just well. However, there's no danger in utilizing both of them since you can't deactivate or remove the Galaxy Store.

HOW TO MAKE PHONE CALL FROM YOUR SAMSUNG GALAXY

Any smartphone, no matter how advanced or beautiful, is essentially a phone. The great thing about the Samsung Galaxy S20 is how simple it is to make and receive calls.

The Galaxy call setup

Making a phone call requires turning on your device and connecting it to your cellular provider. The Home screen is where it all begins. There are four or five main shortcut icons down the screen's bottom, above the Device Function buttons. The main shortcuts on your phone can be a little different, but in this example, they are Phone, Camera, Email, and Messages.

Links on the main screen The main shortcuts are seen on the home screen.

Simply follow these instructions to make a call:

Smartphone symbol

1. Select the Phone icon from the Home screen. This is the kind of screen you might expect to see. The "Recent" tab displays all incoming and

outgoing calls, including the one from your carrier verifying proper phone setup.

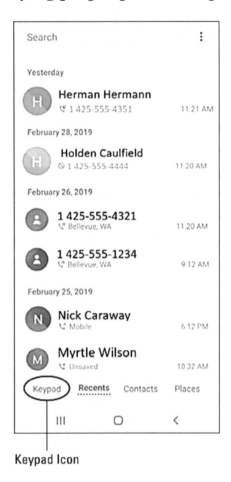

Keypad Icon

The screen of the Galaxy phone's primary display.

2. Select the Keypad icon located in the lower-left corner of your screen. A typical landline phone's touch pad is represented by this icon, which is a green circle with little white dots.

182

3. Select the desired phone number by tapping on it. You will see the Keypad screen. This seems to be a larger-than-life replica of the touch pad seen on conventional landline telephones.

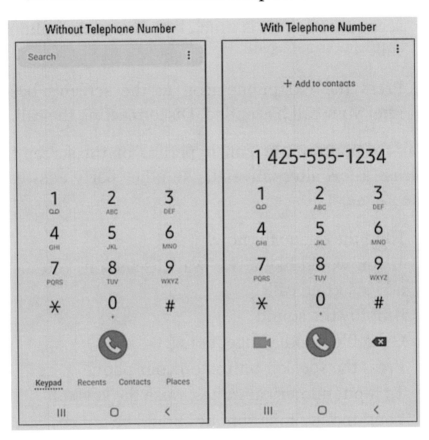

Samsung touchscreen Use the keypad screen to dial the number.

4. Press the green phone icon located at the screen's base to initiate the call. The displayed screen

takes over. You may check whether you reached the desired number.

You should be able to hear either a busy signal or the other party's phone ringing within a few seconds. The rest is much like every other phone call.

5. Press the red phone icon at the screen's base after your call has ended. Disconnecting the call.

Tap the appropriate icon/hyperlink on the screen to access a few alternatives if the other party answers the phone:

- Hold the queue for now.
- If you would like a two-way discussion, you may add a second call.
- Amplify the sound.
- Get a Bluetooth gadget going.
- Press the speaker button on your phone.
- To input numerical values, raise the keypad.
- Your phone's microphone should be muted.

Feel free to pick and choose from these activities or just have a pleasant phone conversation.

Either your area does not have enough cellular service or you accidentally put your phone into Aero plane mode, which disables all of its radios, so the call does not go through. (Of course, your cellphone provider may have allowed you to go without setting up service, but that's very improbable.)

Verify the alerts tab located on the screen's upper edge. Try relocating to a different area if you are unable to see connection-strength bars. Simply pull down the notification screen, locate the aircraft symbol, and press it to disable Aero plane mode if you happen to see a little aero plane silhouette.

Tips for using the Galaxy phone feature

Even more so than placing a call, receiving one is a breeze. A pop-up screen will show you the caller ID whenever someone phones you. A few alternatives for handling an incoming call are shown in this illustration.

Full Screen Incoming call   Partial Screen Incoming call

Getting a phone call Potential greeting displays when a call is incoming.

It will show you the whole screen if you aren't currently using the phone for anything. A pop-up screen, like the one on the right, will appear while you're using an app. Pressing or gliding the green phone button will answer the call. To ignore a call, either press and hold the red phone button or just turn off your phone's ringer. In any event, the ringing ceases instantly, and the call is sent to voicemail.

The respond pop-up screen could display even if you were in the middle of doing anything else on your phone, such as playing a game or listening to music. Until the call ends, you won't be able to play any media, including music or videos.

Callers will need to set up your voicemail before they can leave you a message. A prerecorded message will inform the caller that your voicemail account is not yet configured if you have not yet done so. When you activate your account and get your phone, some cellular providers will automatically set up voicemail; however, with other carriers, you will need to do it yourself. Visit a carrier shop or go to the handbook that came with your phone to learn more about voicemail.

On each mobile device, you may find the usual answer and reject icons. The Galaxy S20 is not your average phone, however. A third option is available, the outcome of which is phone-specific. On top of the usual answer/reject choices, you now have the option to reject the call and text the sender instead. You have the option to send a quick text message to the caller as they are sent to your voicemail, confirming their call.

The following are examples of common pre-written messages:

- Apologies, but I'm occupied at the moment. Return your call at a later time.
- The meeting has begun.
- My phone will ring again.
- At the movie theatre right now.
- It is now class time for me.

To respond, just touch the appropriate message. The caller will know that you aren't ignoring them; you're just unable to speak at this time since the message is delivered immediately as a text. The finishing touch is perfect.

Personal messages like "Please, go away from me" or "I am too busy to talk to you right now" are also available for creation and storage. Being courteous is another option. Tapping Compose new message allows you to easily construct your pre-written message. After that, it is saved on your phone for later use.

The person making the call must have the capability to receive text messages on the phone they are using. This function will not function if the person contacting you is using a landline or a mobile phone that is unable to receive text messages.

SOLUTIONS FOR SAMSUNG GALAXY PHONES THAT FAIL TO MAKE OR TAKE CALLS

Do you find yourself asking, "Why can't I make or receive calls on my Samsung phone?" There are a lot of possible explanations for it. Your phone may be running an out-of-date version of Samsung One UI, you may be in a location with poor network reception, or you may have chosen the incorrect cellular network or mode. For whatever reason, you will find this article useful. When your Samsung Galaxy phone stops making or receiving calls, there are a few things you may do.

Switch Off Your Device.

First things first: reset your Samsung Galaxy phone if you're having trouble making or receiving calls. If this easy remedy doesn't work, try adjusting a few more settings.

Verify Your Network

Finding out whether you have a network is the next step. If your Samsung phone isn't working, it's probably because there isn't a cellular network in your location. Keep an eye out for the status bar's network icon. The network's quality is indicated by the number of bars. You may expect superior quality with a higher number.

Verify Your Cellular Service

If your prepaid or postpaid cell plan has expired or if you haven't paid your monthly expenses, you may be unable to make or receive calls on some networks. Make that your cell plan is active and that you have paid all the fees.

Disable Aero plane Mode

Your Samsung phone may have inadvertently entered airplane mode, also known as Flight mode, which prevents you from making or receiving calls. If you're not familiar, with your phone's cellular network and all other network-related services will be disabled when you go to Aero plane mode.

Toggle off the "Flight mode" option in Settings > Connections. Find out how to remove your Samsung Galaxy phone from airplane mode if you can't get it to exit.

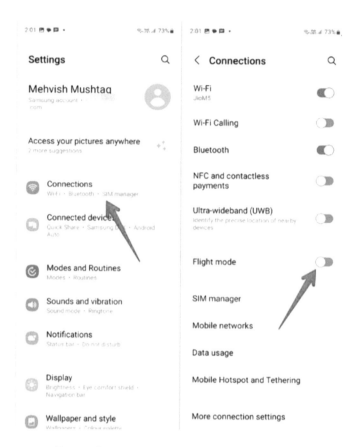

Remove the Phone App's Cache and Data.

If your Samsung phone is having trouble making or receiving calls, clearing the app's cache and data is another tried-and-true method.

Here are the steps to fulfill your request:

1. Go into your Samsung Galaxy phone's settings.
2. Access the Apps panel.
3. Find "Phone" and touch on it.

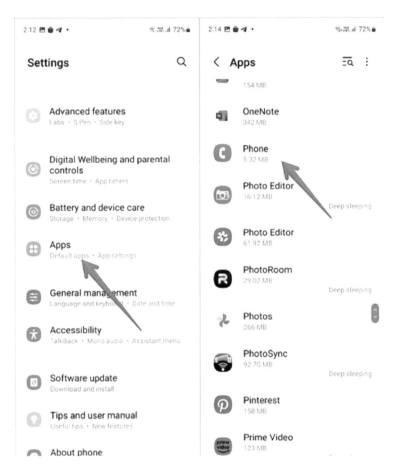

4. Select Storage, and then click the Clear data and Clear cache icons. Power down your device. Just because you clean the cache or data of an app on your phone doesn't mean all of your data and files will be gone. Just the temporary cache files will be deleted. Nevertheless, when you erase all data, the Phone app's settings will be back to the default.

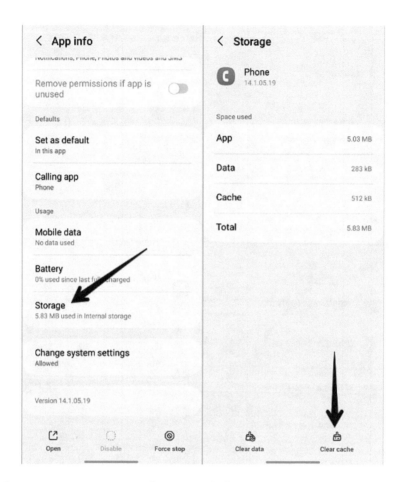

Choose a Network Provider.

Only by connecting your SIM to the network operator that originally provided it will you be able to make and receive calls. You must verify and choose the same network in the operator's settings. Even while it usually happens automatically with Samsung phones, it's still a good idea to double-check everything by hand.

1. Go to your phone's settings.
2. Select Mobile networks from the Connections menu.

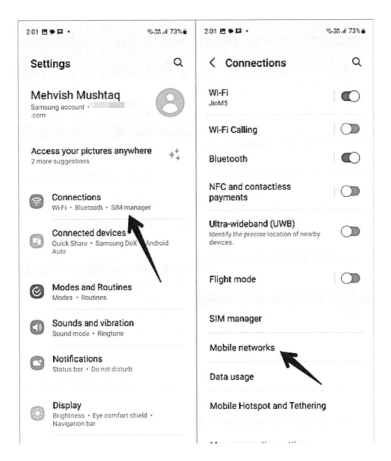

3. Select Network operators. Choose your service provider. Allowing your phone to choose the network automatically is the safest and most optimal choice. Make sure the switch next to "Select automatically" is turned on for that.

4. Put your Samsung Galaxy phone into restart mode.

Switch Network On/Off

Your phone has to be utilizing the right network mode (5G, LTE, 4G) and the right network operator. As an example, 3G is no longer supported by several network carriers. Therefore, you will not be able to make or receive calls on your Samsung phone when it is set to 3G.

What follows are the procedures to change the network mode on a Samsung Galaxy phone:

1. Open the Settings menu on your Samsung Galaxy phone. Then, choose Connections. Finally, tap on Mobile networks.

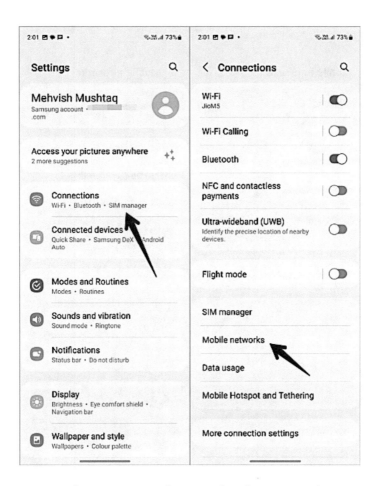

2. Access the Network mode by tapping on it. Figure out which mode is right. Choose the most recent one that says "auto connects" for safety.

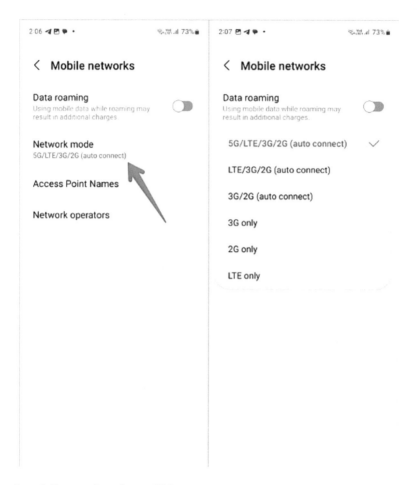

Disable Wi-Fi Calling

Some new features are more trouble than they're worth at times. One of them is Wi-Fi calling, particularly if it interferes with normal calling. If your Samsung phone is having trouble making or receiving calls, you may need to disable Wi-Fi calling.

Toggle off the Wi-Fi calling option in Settings > Connections.

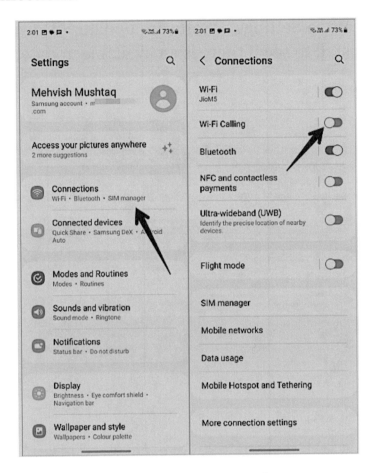

Install the latest software version

When your Samsung Galaxy phone stops making or receiving calls, it's usually because you're using an old version of OneUI. You are obligated to upgrade the OneUI software to the most recent version as soon as it becomes available.

Navigate to Settings > Software update > Download and install to see if there is an available update.

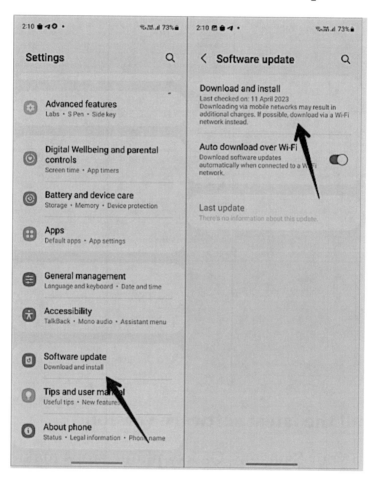

Put the SIM back in

Taking out and replacing the SIM card in your Samsung Galaxy phone may be necessary if none of the preceding solutions work. This method is renowned for its ability to repair issues connected to networks, much like restart.

Clear All Network Preferences

In the end, resetting the network settings should fix your Samsung Galaxy phone's call-making and - receiving issues. Resetting the network to factory settings is what this will do. The data associated with any Wi-Fi networks you have stored or Bluetooth devices you have linked will be erased. Your phone's files and data, however, will remain unaffected.

1. On a Samsung phone, go to the Settings menu, then General Management, and finally, Reset.

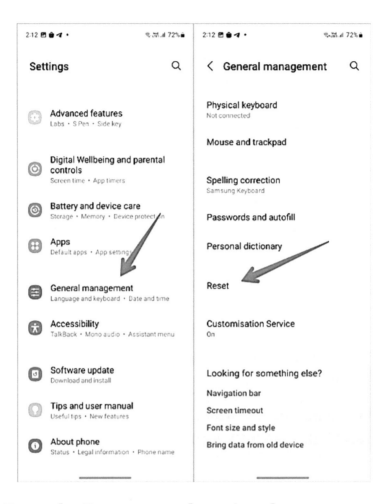

2. Press the Reset network settings button.

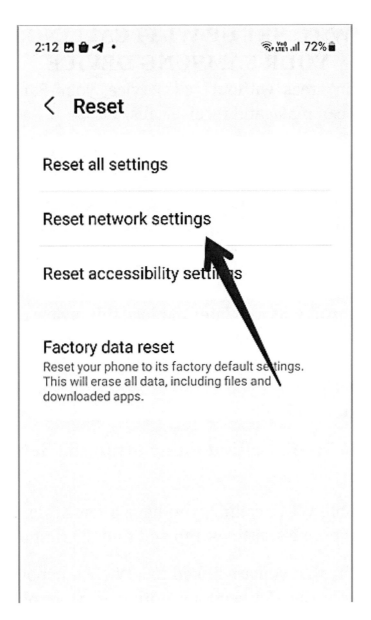

Tips: If that doesn't work, try clearing all of your phone's settings.

HOW TO SET UP WI-FI CALLING ON YOUR SAMSUNG DEVICE

Even in areas without cell service, your Samsung phone can make and receive calls.

- After you've established a Wi-Fi connection, activate Wi-Fi calling by going to Settings > Connections and tapping the corresponding option.
- You may also turn on Wi-Fi calling by opening the Phone app and going to Settings.

For Samsung S5 and later models, this article details the process of making calls using a Wi-Fi network as opposed to the phone's network. On certain other Android phones, you could also find the option to activate Wi-Fi calling.

Toggle Wi-Fi Calling on or off in the Settings Menu

To enable Wi-Fi calling, you have a few options. Go to your phone's settings app and find the first one.

1. Verify that you are linked to a Wi-Fi hotspot.
2. Locate the Connections option in your phone's settings.
3. Press the toggle that appears beside Wi-Fi Calling.

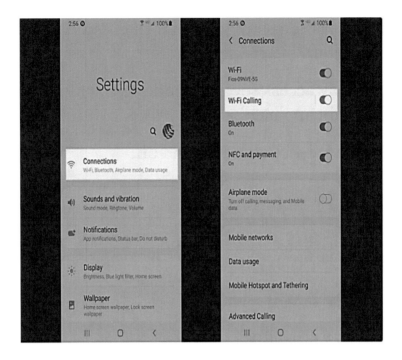

This device's Wi-Fi calling and Connection settings

Instructions for Enabling Wi-Fi Calling on the Mobile App

The Phone app also provides an alternative method of activating this function. To activate it, just follow these steps.

The specifics of these procedures may differ somewhat based on the make and model of your phone as well as the OS you're using.

1. Select Phone from the main menu of your mobile device.

2. To access the settings, press the options icon (or the menu).

   You may access several phone settings right from the main app page.

3. Switch Wi-Fi Calling on and off.

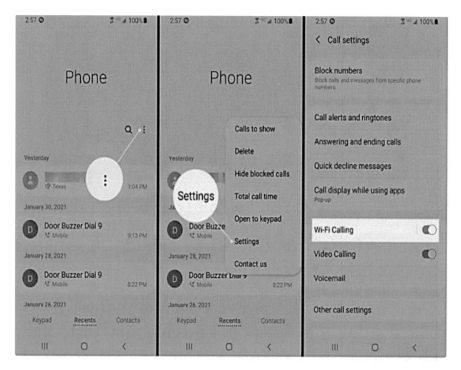

Wi-Fi calling, the Phone app's Settings, and the More menu

Wi-Fi Calling: What Is It?

Instead of using your regular phone network, Wi-Fi calling will allow you to make calls using your wireless network. When you're in a place with decent Wi-Fi but poor phone coverage, or if you have sporadic phone service at home, it may be a lifesaver.

Calling over Wi-Fi wasn't always a good idea because of how unreliable Wi-Fi connections used to be. There aren't many drawbacks to making calls via Wi-Fi, but a few problems may arise. Wi-Fi calling will consume your data plan, which means it might eat into your modest data restriction if you have one for wireless data use.

Another reason to worry about a poor wifi connection is the increased likelihood of dropping calls. In most cases, a strong signal is required for Wi-Fi calling to work.

A simple Skype conversation will be the extent of the data used. Unless your data limit is really low or your use is extremely high, it shouldn't be a problem.

CHAPTER EIGHT

HOW TO BLOCK CALL WITH THE SAMSUNG GALAXY

Every possible way to protect your Galaxy phone from spam and unsolicited calls

In addition to being a lifeline in an emergency or just a nice way to check in with loved ones, phone calls may be annoying and intrusive. Calls from unknown numbers or unsolicited communications may be annoying and, in the worst-case scenario, terrifying. Call blocking is useful in this situation.

The Samsung Galaxy S23 and other highly regarded Samsung phones make it simple to block undesired contacts' calls and texts. To stop telemarketers, fraudsters, and spammers from contacting you frequently to sell you something or steal your personal information, you may set your phone to block unsolicited calls. Also, blocking a number is a discreet technique to stop acquaintances who are a bother from contacting you again if they phone you too often.

Read on if you're confused about how to deactivate a call on a Samsung Galaxy phone. This tutorial will show you all the potential approaches and teach you how to do it step by step.

Identify and block a caller from your call logs

You can stop the number from contacting you again if you have recently received unsolicited calls. For this task to be completed:

1. See who recently called you by opening the Phone app.
2. Choose the relevant phone number.
3. From the menu that appears, choose "info" (i).
4. Select more (the menu symbol with three dots in the bottom right corner).
5. Click on Block contact.

In the absence of a stored contact, you are not obligated to use the More choices button. Instead, the Block button will appear when you touch the I symbol, shortening the distance by one click.

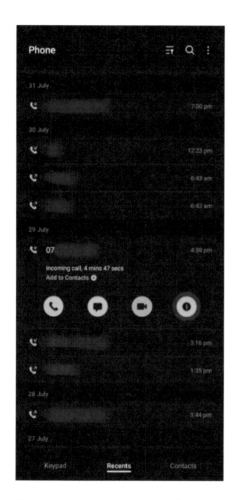 

Remove a contact from your Samsung Phone that you haven't saved

Eliminate a contact's number from your contact list

If you have unwanted phone numbers stored on your Android device, Google account, or SIM card, you may ban them using the Contacts app. I'll show you:

1. Start up the Contacts app.
2. Find the contact whose access you want to revoke.
3. Press the triangle icon (More).
4. Click on Block contact.
5. To confirm, tap Block.

If you want to stop a stored contact from calling you, you may do so by blocking them. Their presence in your Contacts list remains unchanged. You will need to erase the number if you want it gone permanently. You won't be able to unblock a banned contact only by deleting it.

You may disable a certain number in the phone app's settings.

You may block numbers that have phoned you lately or are saved on your device using the techniques mentioned above. The Phone app's settings are where you should go if you want extra choices, such as barring people who have never used your line.

1. Open the app on your phone.
2. Select More by tapping the menu icon (the three dots on the top right).

3. Click on Settings.
4. Select Block numbers from the list's uppermost option.
5. To start blocking, type the number and then hit the + symbol next to it.

Another option is to block a line in your call log. You may also find the option to block a number in your contact list. Toggle a switch to prevent the phone app from contacting private or unknown numbers.

Remove contacts from your Messages list

You may also get unsolicited text messages in addition to robocalls. When this happens, you may use the Google Messages app on your Galaxy mobile to ban the contact:

1. Read Messages.
2. Find the contact whose message you want to block, and then tap and hold the text next to their name.
3. In the top right corner, tap on More choices.
4. Go to Block.
5. To mark the mail as spam, you must decide. Mark it as needed or deselect it.
6. Choose the "OK" button.

If you're using an earlier Samsung Galaxy phone and the default messaging app is Samsung Messages, the mileage may be somewhat different. Here is an alternative approach:

1. Launch Messages on your Samsung device.
2. To block a certain number, find its conversation and click on it.
3. Click on the name (or number) that appears at the top of the screen.
4. Use the drop-down option to choose the Block number.
5. You may choose to remove the discussion from your record. If such is the case, then choose it.
6. To confirm, tap Block.

You can also do the same thing by going to the Samsung Messages settings, tapping Block numbers and spam, and then Block numbers.

The Contacts tab is located at the very bottom of the Samsung Messages app, which you may access via the Conversations tab. If you've saved the number to your contacts, you may now block it just like in the Contacts app.

Look up banned numbers and messages.

When you want to maintain vigilance, what options do you have? If you've sent certain digits to the bottom of the abyss using the block button and can't recall them, you may easily see them again. I'll show you:

1. Open the app on your phone.
2. In the top right corner, tap on More choices.
3. Click on Settings.
4. Pick out the blocks.

Use the page's settings to add people's names as well. Alternately, you might unlink some contacts so they can contact you again.

Samsung Messages also gives you the option to see the list of people you've banned.

1. To get more choices, use the app.
2. Press on Settings.
3. Select Block for numbers and spam.
4. Scroll down to the Block numbers. Instead, choose banned messages if you'd want to see the texts you've banned.

The Block list functions similarly to the Phone app in that it allows you to add or delete contacts or messages.

Unblock individuals or their calls

You can unblock stored numbers in the Contacts app just as you may unblock contacts in the display list. For this purpose:

1. Create a contact.
2. Find and choose the digit.
3. Press on For More.
4. Select the option to unblock contact.

Put an end to unnecessary calls

Spam calls from telemarketers, scammers, fraudsters, and the like are something that everyone gets. Using Samsung's Smart Call function, you may block or report these calls. Unknown calls are automatically identified and classified as potential spammers or fraudsters by the service. The system then gives you the option to take targeted measures either during or after the conversation to address the issue in the best way possible. Certain areas do not have access to the service. Please note that access to this feature is limited to certain carriers, models, and software versions. If you meet the requirements, you may activate it as follows:

1. Launch your phone's app.
2. Slide the menu to see further choices.
3. Click on Settings.

4. Toggle on the feature that blocks unwanted calls and spam.

A Block/Report number option will appear at the bottom of the screen when your phone calls. During or after the call, you have the option to choose one of them. Select "General Spam," "Scam or Fraud," or "Telemarketer" to classify a given number when reporting it. Along the way, you have the option to write a remark.

Depending on your carrier, model, and software version, you may not be able to utilize Samsung's Smart Call function.

Manage who has access to you and who does not

The days of silently accepting obnoxious phone calls and texts are over. Just follow these instructions on your Samsung Galaxy phone to stop those bothersome telemarketers, fraudsters, or bothersome friends from bothering you.

There are times when it's best to just record calls and other times when it's necessary to block them. For instance, you could find it useful to capture a meaningful discussion with a loved one or coworker for reference purposes.

HOW TO LAUNCH THE MESSAGES APP ON YOUR GALAXY DEVICE

The Samsung Galaxy Message app

Use the Messages app on your Galaxy phone or tablet to stay in touch with all of your contacts. Saying hello, sending emoticons, or sharing images has never been simpler. You may silence chats or set unique message tones for certain contacts—just a few of the many things you can do with texts.

the Samsung Messages app, which is compatible with Samsung smartphones running Android 9.0 Pie or later, is the focus of the following features and instructions. No mention of carriers or third-party applications is made in these guidelines. You may only send and receive texts using LTE networks.

Many message formats

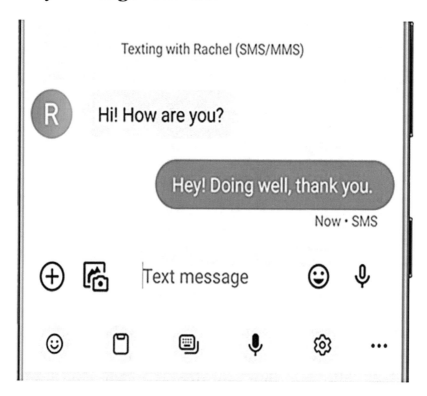

Got a text message discussion

To help you better comprehend the Samsung Messages app, we'll go over the two main message formats.

- Sending and receiving text messages to and from other phones or email addresses is made possible using the Short Message Service (SMS). Subscribing to your provider's messaging service may be necessary for you to use this function.
- Sending and receiving multimedia messages (pictures, videos, and music) to and from other phones or email addresses is possible using the Multimedia Messaging Service (MMS). You may have to sign up for your provider's multimedia messaging service before you can utilize this feature.

The symbols that show up at the top of your screen when messages are received are for messaging.

Message creation and transmission

Curious about tonight's plans? Communicate with your team in a flash. Here you may find instructions on how to compose and send mails.

Messages are automatically preserved as drafts if you quit them before sending them.

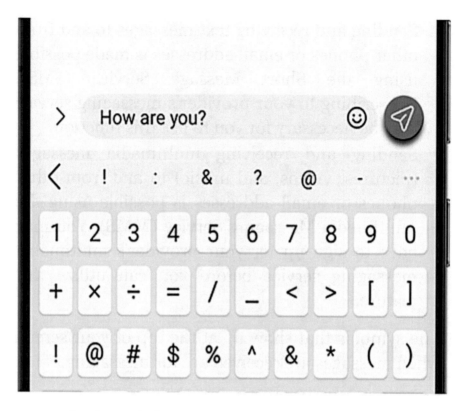

Press the "Send" button on your Messages app.

1. After opening the Messages app, go to the bottom right and hit the Compose symbol. An earlier chat is also accessible by tapping on it.
2. Find the one or ones you want to give it to. You have the option to input a contact's name or phone number.
3. Put your message into text. Select the Gallery or Camera icons located to the left of the text box if you want to include an attachment. If you have

already input any text, you may have to press the arrow adjacent to the box to continue.

Extra attachment choices may be accessed by tapping the plus sign (Add).

4. Use the arrow icon to send your message after you're done.

Make and arrange a message

Everything you need to create the ideal welcome is right there in Messages, including the ability to pre-schedule messages.

A collection of animated GIFs using the Scheduled message

1. Launch Messages on your mobile device. Locate the Compose icon in the bottom right corner.
2. After choosing the receiver(s), hit the Enter message area. Jot down your words.
3. Press the addition symbol (Add). Use the left-hand arrow to go to the + symbol if you can't see it.
4. Pick "Schedule message" next. You may choose the time and date that you would want your text message sent. A maximum of one year from the present day is allowed. Press the Done button when you're done. Select "Set schedule later" if you'd rather.

Any message that you leave before sending will be marked as a draft.

Check for fresh messages

Messages are waiting for you; respond promptly! New messages may be seen in two ways.

Reminder for messages

- Simply scroll down from the top of the screen until you see the Notification panel, and then touch on the New message notification to access your messages.
- Just launch the Messages app, find the discussion containing the new message, and then touch on it to see the new message.
- With the new Bubbles feature enabled, you can now see your messages in a chat window that pops up.

- Press the Play button to start playing the audio or video that was attached to your message.

Make use of group chats.

If you want to communicate with many individuals, you may do so by creating group messages in the Samsung Messages app. Group communications also allow the sending of images and videos, making it simpler to communicate information with several people at once.

Sending a message to all Galaxy phone users saying, "Hey everyone!"

Personalization of messages

Samsung has you covered when it comes to adding flair to your handset. You may change the theme of your phone to make your Messages app seem the way you want it to.

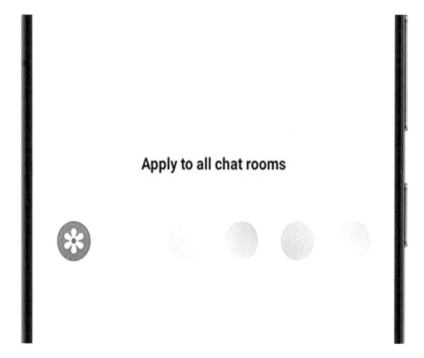

Choose your ringtone for message thread notifications.

Make the necessary adjustments to your font settings if you want to alter the font used by Messages.

For each thread in a conversation, you may also choose a different background color or wallpaper. Select more choices (the three vertical dots) from the discussion you want to edit, and then choose Customize background or Customize chat room. You may pick a picture from the gallery by tapping the icon, or you can change the backdrop color by tapping a color. Altering the text contrast and bubble opacity is also possible on some devices.

Personalized ringtones for various contacts

Options for a discussion using the "Notification Sound" icon

If you want to instantly recognize whether it's your mom or your closest buddy who messages you, you may select personalized ringtones for various contacts.

Navigate to the discussion you want to see by opening Messages on your mobile device. After you've tapped the three vertical dots that represent further choices, choose Notification sound. After that, choose the sound you want to hear once that chat is over.

Now, whenever a new message arrives, the one you choose will play, and the Messages app will display a badge with a number representing the number of unread messages.

Your carrier and the status of your service may affect the notification settings on your mobile device.

Handle classifications

To make finding certain messages simpler, you may organize them into different Conversation categories. To illustrate the point, suppose you and your buddies use many group chats and you'd want to maintain tabs on them all. You may easily organize your mails by creating a few categories.

1. Get the Messages app, open it, and then hit the three vertical dots for More choices.
2. Select Settings from the menu. To enable Conversation categories, touch the corresponding option.
3. Press on Conversation Categories after that.

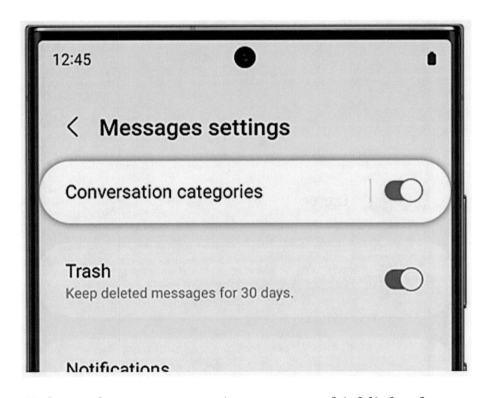

Galaxy phone conversation category highlighted

4. After you've entered the name you'd like for the category, press Add.
5. You may add chats to a category by tapping the search box on the next page and then searching for them.
6. Going back to Messages, you can see your new category by clicking on its name up top. Find the "Add conversations" button. Tap Done after selecting the discussions you want to include in that category.

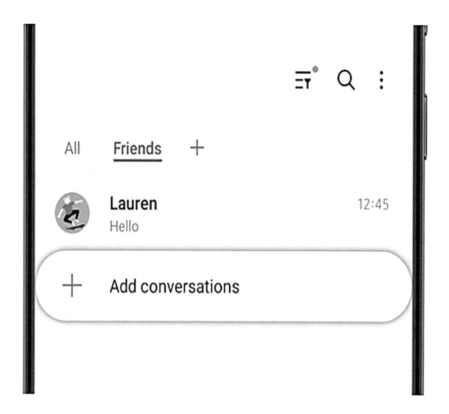

In the Messages app, you may rename conversations and add new ones.

7. Tap More choices (the three vertical dots), then choose Edit categories. Then, touch and hold the category you want to eliminate. At the very bottom, tap on Delete or Delete all.
8. The Conversation categories page makes it simple to see certain categories or locate specific conversations. Everything will be conveniently organized in one spot.

Diagonalizable the text size

The second message is bigger than the first in the text message.

You wish the font was larger so you could read your messages word by word, but it's too little. You may change the font size of certain messages independently of your device's default setting.

Launch the Messages app, find the message you want to read, and then squeeze to zoom in or out using two fingers. Adjusting the size of the typeface is an automated process. Only the messages seen in the Messages app will be affected by your modifications, and the size you choose will be kept until you make another change.

Modify your profile image

Personalize your messages by uploading a photo to your profile in the Messages app. Either use the icons that are included in the program or upload your own.

1. Locate and launch the Contacts app from the Home screen. Above your Contacts, you'll see your profile.
2. Go to your profile by tapping the top icon, then Edit, and finally Gallery.
3. To set your photo as your profile image, click on the photo. Another option is to use the Camera app to snap a picture or choose a pre-made icon.

Customize the contact's profile page using picture editing tools

4. Before hitting "Done," crop the image. (Cropping an icon is not possible.) Your profile page also has the option to be edited or added to.
5. Select Save to commit your changes. If the person you're contacting uses a Samsung phone, they'll be able to view your profile image.

Other people can't see your icon unless you enable profile sharing on your phone.

Turn conversation alerts on or off

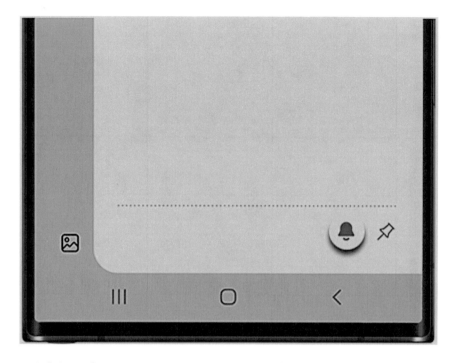

Within the Messages app, a blue bell is shown beside a thumb tac.

Notifications are sent to you whenever a contact messages you, as a default setting. However, if you're in the middle of a meeting and would prefer not to be interrupted, you have the option to mute the whole chat.

To access more choices in a chat, open Messages, choose the conversation and then press the three vertical dots. The arrangement of the mute option may vary from carrier to carrier; for example, you may need to touch the Bell symbol or Mute Conversation. Press the bell symbol or Unmute Conversation again to turn off the sound.

The Bell symbol will show as blue while the conversation is not muted and as clear as it is. Although you will not get alerts when new texts come, you are still able to see them even when a conversation is muted.

Eliminate chat history messages

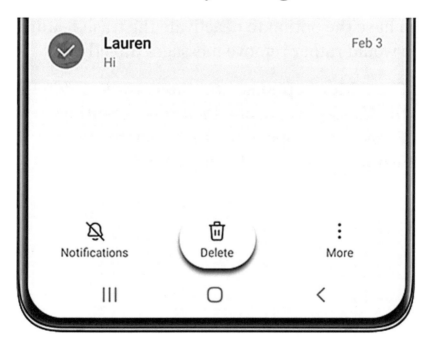

Find the discussion you want to read by opening the Messages app.

Clear up your inbox of any outdated messages that are taking up space. The storage on your phone will be great.

1. To remove a message, press and hold it until you see the Delete button. Selecting all messages is also possible by tapping All.
2. To confirm, tap Move to Trash. The message will be kept in the Trash for 30 days.
3. Messages app's "Move to Trash" feature

Eliminate Message Trash

You have the option to deactivate the trash feature if you would rather remove messages directly.

1. Press More options (the three vertical dots) on the Messages app, and then choose Settings.
2. Press the toggle next to Trash to disable the feature. When asked, tap Turn off.

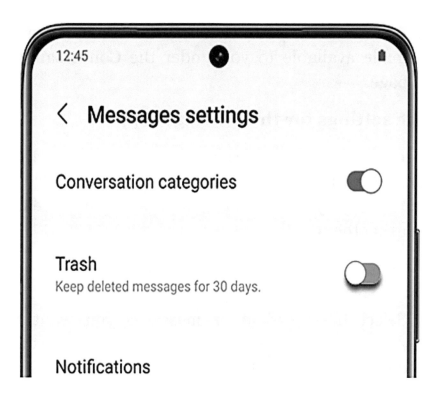

Disabled the trash option in the Messages settings.

3. Just press the switch again to turn it back on at a later time.

Find lost texts in the trash

Within thirty days, you may retrieve a message that you erased inadvertently from the Trash.

1. Select more choices (the three vertical dots) on the Messages app, and then choose Trash.
2. To restore a single message or all of them, touch and hold the one you want to restore.

3. Rest assured, your chat will be recovered and made available to you under the Conversations page.

The settings for the Messages app

In case you were unaware of them, the Messages app has some helpful options and functions. Make better use of your messaging and texting experience by using them.

- To locate a certain thread of messages, just click the Search button.
- Select the message or messages you want to delete by touching and holding them. To ensure deletion, press Move to Trash after tapping Delete or Delete all at the bottom. Going to the Conversations tab, tapping More choices (the three vertical dots), and finally tapping Trash will allow you to retrieve a message that you accidentally erased. For each message, press and hold until you get the option to restore it individually or all of them at the bottom.
- To star or favorite a conversation bubble, just press and hold it. Then, hit Star message. Press More choices (the three vertical dots) on the Conversations page, then press Starred messages

to see the messages that have been marked as favorites.

- Remove undesirable communications: You have the option to remove or ban messages. Choose the Block number at the beginning of the discussion if you get a suspicious SMS. Select More options (the three vertical dots), then select Settings, from which you may see banned numbers and messages or even block a number. This is located in the Conversations tab. Select Block for numbers and spam.

- You can "pin" a chat by going to the conversation's menu (three vertical dots), tapping "More options," and then tapping the "pin" symbol down at the bottom. This discussion will now take precedence over any other messages that have not been pinned.

- Get the latest version of the app: Select More choices (the three vertical dots) from the Conversations tab. Then, choose Settings. Finally, touch on About Messages. To install an update, just hit the Update button.

- You may logically arrange your interactions by creating categories. More information may be found in the "Manage categories" section.

- In the "Notifications" section, you may choose how you want messages to be notified. To access the notification sound, go to the message and press the three vertical dots (More choices).

- Critical situation settings: Go over all of your previous emergency notifications.

Keyboard functions

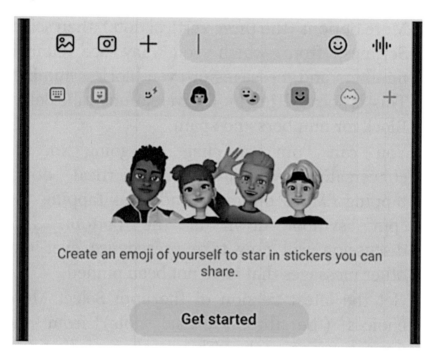

Create an emoji of yourself to star in stickers you can share.

Get started

Adding personalized emojis and emoji stickers to your texts is a great way to spice up your chats. Other features include voice-activated message writing, language customization for the keyboard, and the ability to configure smart typing capabilities like auto-replace and predictive text. To make message creation and sending even simpler, you may customize these features.

HOW TO USING THE SAMSUNG PHONE'S CAMERA

Learn the ropes of your Samsung Galaxy phone's camera with this simple and fast tutorial.

Because there are so many choices to choose from when snapping a picture, modern smartphone camera settings may be a bit of a pain to manage. Compared to other phones, Samsung Galaxy phones provide more camera options; thus, let's go over the fundamentals of the camera so that you can make the most of it.

Taking a picture of the primary screen of the Samsung camera

Screenshots of the Samsung camera's modes and Snapchat filters

Getting to know the many capture modes on your Samsung camera is the first step in mastering its operation.

Above the capture button (the large white circle) on your Samsung phone, you'll find a row of settings that you may scroll through to customize how you shoot images or videos.

The most fundamental Video and Photo choices, along with a Portrait option, are located in this row, but that's not all. Panorama, Night, Single Take, and Slow Motion are among the other capture kinds that become available when you scroll down and press the More option. When you're taking photos of your food, you may even choose the "Food" option.

All it takes to snap a picture is aligning your subject with the screen and tapping the Capture button once you've chosen your preferred choice.

Two more choices, Bixby Vision and AR Zone, are included under the extended capture modes. The first of these two functions is a virtual assistant, and it is specific to Samsung.

Bixby is a helpful assistant that can access applications, make calls, and seek information. Moreover, using Bixby Vision, you can translate text, scan QR codes, and even find things to purchase online all using your phone's camera. You can add drawings, avatars, and other augmented reality components to your images using Samsung's AR Zone.

On the leftmost side of the main row of choices, depending on your phone's model and operating system version, you could also notice a Fun category. Using Snapchat Lenses, this function gives you access to a variety of effects that might let you experiment with your photos a little.

The Flash, the Timer, and Other Camera Functions

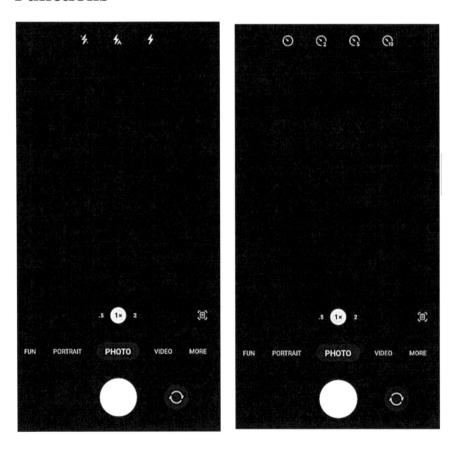

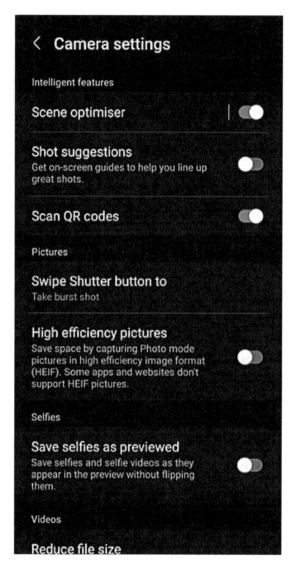

Take a screenshot of the settings for my Samsung camera, including the flash, timer, and general settings.

At the very top of your Samsung camera screen, you'll see a bar that gives you access to additional camera functions. As a bonus, it has a customizable timing and two flash modes: automatic and manual.

The lightning bolt-shaped Flash option lets you choose between a manual, always-on flash, an automated flash that kicks in when the light becomes dim, or a full flash-off.

You may insert yourself into a group shot by setting a two-, five---, or ten-second timer using the Timer function, which appears as a clock. The timer may, of course, be disabled completely if desired.

Squared off next to the play button is the Motion Photo option, which allows you to record a short video clip before taking a picture. It's very much like the live photographs on the iPhone.

Additional functions including video stabilization, QR code scanning, shot recommendations, and grid lines may be accessed by opening the options cog on the left side of this bar.

You may also adjust the aspect ratio of your Samsung camera's captured video or stills. Alternate aspect ratios may be accessed by tapping the 3:4 symbol located at the screen's top. You could notice a little change in the icon's appearance as you adjust the ratio, as the numbers on it will shift.

Lastly, you'll see the Filters tool on the top bar. On the far right side of the bar, you can see an object that resembles a magic wand. Here you may browse through some picture filters, such as black and white, warm tones, and fading effects.

Methods for Increasing and Decreasing Size

You have two options when it comes to adjusting the magnification of your camera. To begin, you have the option to utilize the zoom settings that are supplied at the bottom of the lens view. You may adjust the magnification from half axe to ten times. The specifics of these choices could vary from one phone model to another.

Just put two fingers in the middle of the screen and move them outside to manually zoom. You may zoom in by using this. To zoom out, just do the reverse: put two fingers on the screen at different locations and then bring them together.

Selfie Techniques

To activate the front-facing lens and switch to Selfie mode on your Samsung camera, just hit the rotation symbol (the circular arrows) on the bottom right of the screen.

When compared to the primary camera, the selfie camera is severely lacking in functionality. Take your selfie camera—it doesn't have panoramic, macro, food, or slow motion modes, among other features.

But don't worry; the front-facing camera still has all your favorite modes like Portrait, Night, and Hyperlapse.

The Samsung Galaxy Camera: A User's Guide

It could be difficult to get used to your Samsung camera if you aren't very tech-savvy. Nonetheless, the software is intuitive, and by following the aforementioned instructions, you will be able to master all the capabilities you need to elevate your smartphone photography.

HOW TO CONFIGURE THE CAMERA ON A GALAXY PHONE

Daisy serves as the backdrop for the Galaxy S23 Ultra camera modes screen.

Shooting dynamic photographs and videos is a breeze with Galaxy phones and tablet cameras, which provide a range of shooting modes and settings. Portrait Mode, Director's View, Super Slow-mo, and AR Doodle expand the range of options. Video size and grid lines are two other parameters that you may adjust to improve your photographs.

Not all devices will have access to the same settings.

Set up several types of shots

Not all modes will be available on all devices; in fact, some may need downloading before they can be used. Go to the shooting mode menu:

1. Swiping up from the bottom of the screen will bring up the Apps menu. From there, you can start the Camera app.

Open the camera app.

2. To change modes, swipe either right or left. Here are the available options:
   - Enhances photographs with various backdrop effects for portraiture.
   - Picture: Chooses the best settings automatically.
   - Optimal video settings are selected.
   - Plus: Unveils more shooting modes, letting you personalize them in the tray.
   - Professional Raw and Expert both have the option to manually adjust exposure and ISO.
   - There are specialized settings for several circumstances, such as night, food, panorama, and more.

Despite being compatible with Dual Rec, the Galaxy S24 series does not have a Director's View.

Choose a shooting mode, then position your subject and press the shutter button. For faraway objects, use Space Zoom.

Configuring the camera

Settings menu for the Galaxy phone's camera

Launch the Camera app and go to the Settings menu to access further settings. Functions comprise:

- Smart features: They can auto-scan papers and even identify QR codes.
- Photos and videos: Selectable high-efficiency codecs, HDR10+ recording, and sophisticated stabilization options.

- In general, the shooting experience is improved with the addition of grid lines, location markers, and customizable shooting techniques.

Photographic advice

Here are some ideas for images that will grab people's attention:

- During the golden hour, which occurs soon after dawn and just before sunset, you may capture the warm glow of the sun.
- To improve lighting inside, take advantage of natural light sources, such as windows.

- To achieve more visually appealing compositions, turn on grid lines in the Camera app and use the rule of thirds.
- To get more authentic-looking shots, make sure your subjects are relaxed.

CHAPTER NINE

HOW TO MAKE USE OF GALAXY PHONE FEATURES LIKE LIVE FOCUS OR PORTRAIT MODE

Make use of Galaxy phone features like Live Focus or Portrait mode.

If you're a fan of Samsung's revolutionary cameras, you know they're a blast to use and provide plenty of customization choices to capture the perfect photo. For some time now, Galaxy smartphone cameras have had the Live Focus function, which is renowned for its distinctive filters. On Galaxy smartphones running One UI 4, such as the S21 and S22 series, the original Live Focus is now integrated into Portrait mode, while it remains fantastic. A whole new world of selfie-enhancing filters and effects is at your fingertips in Portrait mode.

The data shown here is exclusive to Galaxy smartphones sold in Canada that are running the latest version of One UI, which is 3. Smartphones sold in different countries could have different screens and options available.

One UI 3 Live Focus

As soon as you activate this function, your selected filter will be applied to the current image. Use the front-facing camera for perfect selfies or the rear-facing camera for breathtaking group shots.

Press MORE after opening the Camera app. Select LIVE FOCUS, and then press the circle in the screen's lower right corner. You may use the slider to change each of the available settings.

- Blur: Live Focus on One UI 3: This will make the surrounding area less sharp.

- Create a concentrated circle around your topic while blurring the backdrop with the big circle effect.
- Colorpoint: Makes the hues immediately around your topic sharper, turning all other colors into black and white.
- By using the zoom feature, you may make it seem as if you are rapidly approaching the topic.
- To make the topic pop out of the backdrop, you may use the spin effect, which spins the subject around.

The One UI 4's portrait mode-mode

Live Focus is now available in portrait mode on the Galaxy S21 and Galaxy S22 series, as well as other phones with One UI 4. Additionally, you have access to extra filters and effects to elevate your photo-taking game. Impressive selfies are within your reach!

Press MORE after opening the Camera app. Hit PORTRAIT, and then press the circle on the right side of the viewfinder's bottom. The slider allows you to change the choices.

After launching the Camera app on the Galaxy S22 series, you'll see the PORTRAIT option at the bottom of the screen.

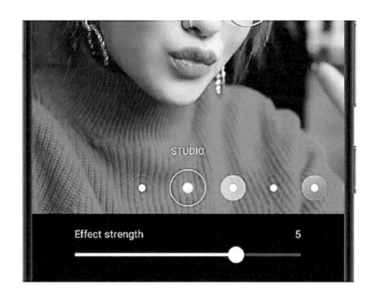

- Portrait mode Blur on One UI 4: Just like Live Focus on older smartphones, this one blurs the backdrop surrounding the subject.
- Studio: This option emphasizes the topic by brightening it without changing the backdrop brightness, creating a striking contrast.
- "High-key mono" means very bright and monochromatic. Everything in the image and on the topic will be seen in monochrome.
- Low-key mono: The same as high-key mono, but with a black-and-white image instead. Nevertheless, it opts for dim lighting instead.
- The backdrop effect uses a gradient to make the surrounding area of the topic seem grey, while the subject itself retains its hue.

- For a more dramatic effect, you may adjust the color point to make the hues immediately around your topic seem darker, drawing attention to it.

Shoot in portrait mode or with live focus.

Regardless of the model of your phone, as long as it has received the One UI 3 or later update, you may use the same settings for Live Focus video and Portrait video, despite their distinct titles. These modes, similar to their image counterparts, apply effects to whatever you're capturing with the front or back cameras.

Press MORE after opening the Camera app. Select either PORTRAIT or LIVE FOCUS VIDEO, and then press the circle in the viewfinder's lower right corner. The slider allows you to change each of the four available choices.

Shoot in portrait mode or with live focus.

- To blur the backdrop surrounding your subject, use the blur function.
- Create a concentrated circle around your topic while blurring the backdrop with the big circle effect.
- Colorpoint: Makes the hues immediately around your topic sharper, turning all other colors into black and white.
- On purpose, this will cause a static, multicolored effect to appear in the backdrop.

HOW DOES SAMSUNG'S SINGLE-TAKE MODE WORK?

Using the Samsung Galaxy phone's Single Take feature, you can always get the ideal shot.

Revolutionary is the Single Take mode seen on Samsung Galaxy smartphones. Quickly and easily capture high-quality images and movies with its assistance. Even while this isn't exactly ground-breaking, the S21 series of smartphones has made several enhancements that make it even more impressive.

Now that we know what the Single Take feature is, let's see how to utilize it effectively.

Definition of "Single Take"

You may snap several images or movies with the single press of a button thanks to the handy Single Take function. Using up to ten seconds of continuous shooting in a variety of modes, your phone records whatever's in the frame. Artificial intelligence then selects and shares the finest shots.

Of all, Single Take isn't a magic bullet if your lighting is terrible or your viewpoint is off. It won't make your images appear flawless and professional. You should still aim for a respectable shot before using Single Take to maximize your potential.

The Single Take function has been enhanced for the current Samsung smartphone generation and was first debuted on the Galaxy S20 series.

An Aesthetic engine and an Angle Evaluation engine have been included in the AI to further enhance your images. With the help of these engines, your phone can detect whether subjects are staring blankly or apply simple filters to your movies and still images.

The most recent S21 devices may have better artificial intelligence for Single Take, but the functionality is still compatible with any Samsung Galaxy phone running Android 10 or later, including:

- The Note 20 series, the S20 series, the Z Fold 2 series, the A51 series, and the A71 series are all included.

Applying Single Take

Launch your camera app to get the Single Take function. You should be able to find Single Take towards the bottom of the screen, where you typically choose between picture and video modes. To turn it on, just swipe over.

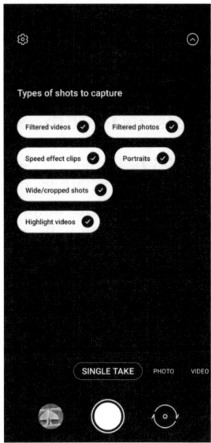

One-shot mode on the Samsung Galaxy, including the ability to preview one-shots in the camera gallery.

You may access the Shot Types menu using the drop-down menu located in the upper right corner of your screen. Selecting the various media formats you want to include in your Single Take shot is as simple as tapping here.

Simply hold your phone in that spot as it takes a photo; that's all it takes when you're ready. If you want better video or other viewpoints, you can even move your phone as the shooting is happening.

Reasons to Utilize Single-Take

When you want to record a memorable moment but aren't sure whether you want still images or moving ones, or if you want to experiment with different lenses and filters, Single Take is the way to go.

With Single Take, you may get the perfect photograph without the hassle of taking the photo by yourself. If you're in awe of a breathtaking scene or an untamed animal but don't have time to carefully consider your photo options, Single Take will save you the trouble and provide you with plenty of options to choose from later.

This is particularly helpful for vacations and special events like birthdays when you want to take plenty of pictures and videos but don't want to deal with the trouble of deciding which angles to use.

Delight in Your Emerging Capacity for Photography

You will be the unofficial photographer at all of your loved ones' big occasions after you learn how to use the Single Take function on your Samsung Galaxy smartphone. No matter how much you like or dislike your new employment, you can always count on your photos and videos to turn out beautifully.

To keep capturing amazing images and movies for a long time, equip your Samsung mobile with screen protectors, a decent case, and other accessories.

TIPS FOR ACTIVATING NIGHT MODE ON SAMSUNG DEVICES

Protect your eyes from harmful blue light with a special filter.

- To switch to night mode, go to the Display menu in the setting. To activate night mode, just tap the toggle. Establish a timetable and discuss available choices.
- Navigate to the Display menu in Settings to enable the blue light filter. To activate the blue light filter, tap the corresponding toggle. Decide on a timetable.
- Manual: The Notifications shade may be slid down. Find Quick Settings by swiping down. Select the blue light filter or night mode.

Learn how to manually activate night mode and the blue light filter on Samsung phones, or create a personalized schedule for each function, in this article.

The Night Mode: How to Use It

You may make your Samsung phone more readable in low light by using either the Samsung blue light filter or the Samsung night mode. You may activate both of them with a simple click in the Quick Settings. In the settings, you have the option to set night mode to open automatically.

1. Navigate to the Display menu in the Settings app.
2. Toggle the Night mode on/off by tapping the corresponding button on the right.
3. Press the "Night mode" button on the left to set the timer for when night mode will activate and deactivate automatically.

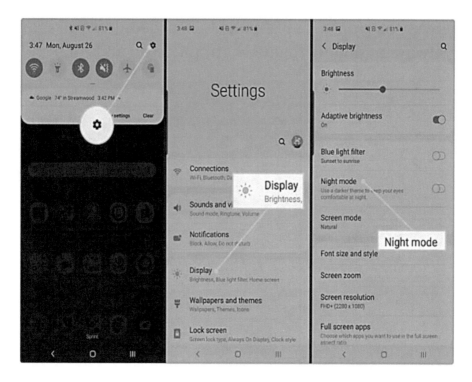

In Samsung Settings, you may access Night mode using the gear icon, display button, and the camera.

4. Choose the switch For Night mode to automatically turn on and off, turn it on as planned.
5. You may customize the time it turns on and off by selecting Sunset to Dawn or Custom Schedule.
6. To modify the start and end timings of a custom schedule, just touch on them.

Even if you've established a schedule, you can always manually toggle Night mode on and off.

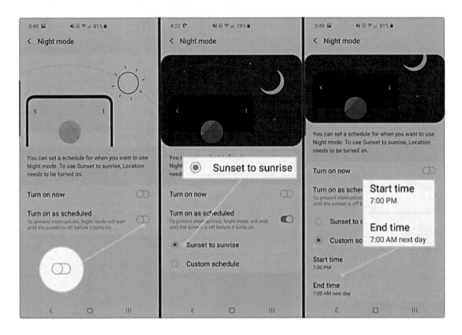

In Night mode, you may specify the time to begin and end the activity, switch from Sunset to Sunrise, and more.

What the Samsung Blue Light Filter Is and How to Use It

The blue light filter is also toggleable in the Settings menu.

1. Navigate to the Display menu in the Settings app.
2. Toggle the Blue light filter on/off using the button on the right.

3. Tap the words "Blue light filter" on the left to set up a daily schedule for turning the filter on and off, and to alter the filter's opacity.

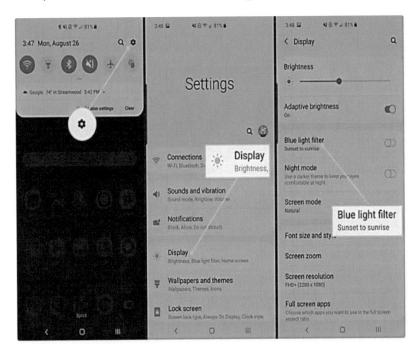

Samsung Settings: Gear icon, Display button, and Blue light filter button

4. With the blue light filter enabled, you may control the amount of blue light that passes through by adjusting the filter's Opacity.
5. Choose Sunset to Dawn or Custom Schedule from the options when you touch Turn on as scheduled to configure the filter to run at certain times each day.

271

6. To configure the times to turn the filter on and off, touch the Start time and End time, respectively, when you pick a custom schedule.

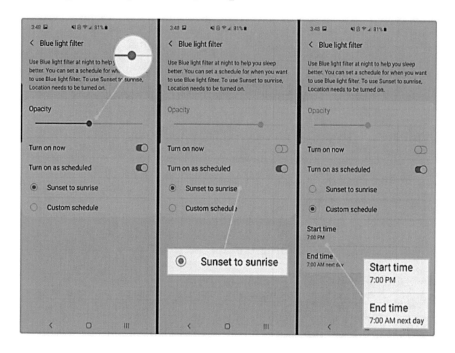

Adjustable opacity Choose the time of day from sunset to dawn Beginning and ending timings in Samsung's settings

Methods for Manually Enabling the Blue Light Filter or Night Mode

Swiping down the Notification shade is the quickest method to activate night mode or the blue light filter. You can access your phone's quick settings by swiping down twice. There, you'll see the icons that allow you to switch on and off services like Wi-Fi, Bluetooth, torch, and more. Find Night mode or the Blue light filter by swiping right; then, press once to activate it. Press it once again to disable it.

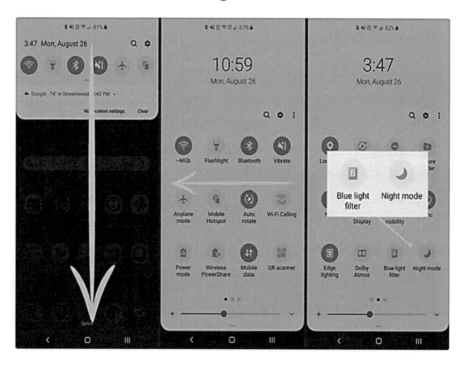

Drag down, drag left, Night mode with a blue light filter icons

Difference Blue Light Filter vs. Samsung's Night Mode

While in night mode, your phone's UI components take on the opposite colors of each other, such as white for black and vice versa. With Android Pie came the night mode, which this makes use of. At night, it may dim your phone's light so it's easier to read. But not every app supports night mode. Some apps don't adhere to night mode's rules; for instance, Amazon Shopping and Samsung Health. In terms of success or failure, it's a real crapshoot.

The screen's output is impacted by the blue light filter. Because it doesn't depend on applications following a rule, it works globally, which is a huge advantage. It doesn't matter what's on your screen; it just decreases blue light output. While the blue light filter won't darken your screen as night mode does, there is some evidence that it could make it easier to fall asleep and improve your sleep quality in general.

Using either mode at nighttime might alleviate eye strain and light sensitivity.

There is a little difference between the night mode that arrived with Android Pie and the blue light filter and mode that Samsung offers. When the sun goes low, they will make your screen easier to read. When you switch to Samsung's night mode, the screen's components are darkened, making the phone's dazzling screen less noticeable in low light. One software option that might help lower your screen's blue light output is the blue light filter.

HOW TO CAPTURE A SCREENSHOT ON A SAMSUNG DEVICE

The ability to capture a screenshot is one of the most helpful features on our smartphones these days, whether we're attempting to preserve some information for later or want to share something we stumbled upon. Fortunately, taking screenshots has been standardized across most Android manufacturers, so you shouldn't have any trouble picking up the skill on a Samsung Galaxy phone. Isn't that a stretch? The steps are below.

The Samsung Galaxy phone's screenshot procedure

With a Samsung phone, you can capture screenshots in three different ways: one is very clear, while the other two are, well, not so much. Below, we'll demonstrate all three of these approaches.

Please be informed that these techniques are compatible with the majority of Samsung Galaxy devices. This includes the Galaxy S, Note, and most recent Galaxy A models from the last four years. The other two methods may not work on phones older than four years; instead, they may only be compatible with the following key combination screenshot technique.

The Samsung phone shortcut for taking a screenshot

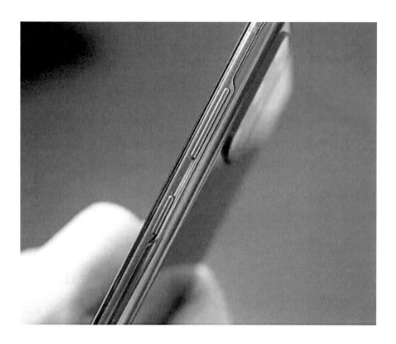

The side keys of the Samsung Galaxy

To capture a rapid screenshot on a Samsung phone, similar to other Android devices, you'll need to master a motion that combines the power button and the volume button. Once you've got the hang of it, however, you won't want to miss a thing.

1. Launch the document whose screenshot you want to capture.
2. Hold down the power and volume buttons simultaneously for one second, then let go.

   Your phone will either lower the volume or initiate a long-press action with the power button if you keep the buttons pressed for more than a second. To capture a screenshot, just press and hold the buttons for one second.

3. Either the notification shade or the bottom bar that appears on the screen (far right button) will allow you to share the screenshot instantly.
4. Pressing the center button also enters an editing mode. You may edit the screenshot by cropping it and adding drawings before saving or sharing it.

Methods for taking screenshots with a palm swipe on Samsung phones

1. To take a screenshot, first open the content.

2. Hold your hand vertically on either side of the phone and, in a single motion, swipe it across the screen, ensuring that your hand remains in touch with the screen.
3. Verify that Palm swipe to capture is enabled in Settings, Advanced features, Motions, and gestures if this solution does not work.
4. The process of saving, sharing, and editing the screenshot remains the same regardless of whether you access it from the on-screen toolbar or the notification shade.

How to take a screenshot with Bixby Voice on a Samsung phone

Using Bixby with Your Galaxy

If you're having trouble holding your phone steady enough to utilize the buttons or palm swipe, you can use Bixby to capture screenshots instead. To take advantage of the function, you must activate Bixby again if you have disabled it.

1. To take a screenshot, first open the content.
2. Once you've launched Bixby Voice, a long press of the button will start it by default.
3. While the interface is active, the command "take a screenshot."
4. The other techniques provide quick editing possibilities, while the Bixby approach does not. But if you want to get fancy, you may phrase your orders like "take a screenshot and share it to Twitter" and so on.

Use "scroll capture" to take additional pictures.

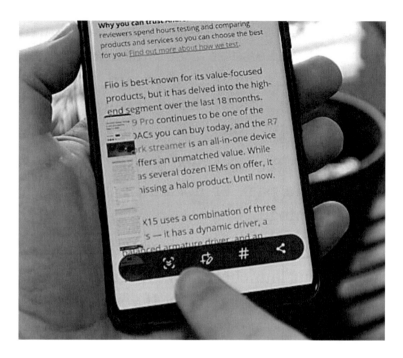

Utilize scroll capture to take screenshots that exceed the height of your screen

After you've captured a screenshot, you'll get a menu with choices, one of which is "screen capture." This is true regardless of how you initiate the capture process. This icon, which appears as a box on the left side of the screen with arrows pointing downwards, allows the user to take many screenshots of the current screen content. These pictures are then combined into a single tall screenshot to display the whole screen. Capturing a whole website, set of detailed instructions, or lengthy restaurant menu is a breeze with this.

No need to press the scroll capture button more than once; it will also stop automatically when you reach the screen's bottom. Afterward, you'll be able to share, modify, or save the screenshot in the same way you would any other.

Holding down the scrolling button allows you to record a whole page or document at once, saving you some tapping.

You can find the Samsung Gallery app in the app drawer of your launcher. From there, you may view your screenshots for later use. If you like to save all of your screenshots in one convenient location, you may access them in the Screenshot album located under the Album tab, in addition to the main camera roll.

Record what's on your screen using any Android

You may choose from some excellent Android phones if you aren't already using one. You can still capture a screenshot quickly on Pixel, for instance, if you go with a Google phone. The Samsung Galaxy S23 Plus, for example, has an excellent camera system and always runs smoothly, making it one of the greatest flagship phones from Samsung. You can be certain that this top-notch device will serve you well for many years to come thanks to the guaranteed four years of platform upgrades and five years of security updates.

CHAPTER TEN

METHODS FOR RECORDING THE SCREEN ON THE SAMSUNG GALAXY A35 5G

Capturing the action on your smartphone screen is a must-have skill in today's environment. Screen recording is a great tool to have on hand whether you want to show off a cool software feature, provide a lesson, or share a gaming highlight.

The Samsung Galaxy A35 5G has a screen recording capability that is sure to be a hit with any user of this smartphone. Consequently, documenting and sharing your mobile experiences has never been easier.

Methods for Recording the Screen on the Samsung Galaxy A35 5G

Launch the Quick Settings and notification panel by swiping down from the top of your screen. Locate the screen recorder icon in the Quick Settings panel when it has been opened. Its appearance is sometimes reminiscent of a little video camera or camcorder.

Capture the Screen on the Samsung Galaxy A35 5G

To start recording your screen, tap the symbol for the screen recorder. Options to change the audio source and other settings may show in a pop-up menu. Press the "Start Recording" button to begin screen recording once you've made your selections.

Capture the Screen on the Samsung Galaxy A35 5G

A toolbar will appear on the screen while you are recording. You may stop the recording completely, switch between the front and back cameras, add notes or drawings to the screen, and more from this toolbar.

Capture the Screen on the Samsung Galaxy A35 5G

After you're done recording, hit the stop button on the toolbar. Your screen recording will be stored in the gallery or anywhere you choose on your device automatically.

You may simply record what's happening on your Samsung Galaxy A35 5G screens and share it with others using the screen recording function. Learning how to screen record may be useful for a variety of reasons, including but not limited to educating yourself, troubleshooting, and recording your mobile experience.

HOW DOES SAMSUNG HEALTH WORK?

Users get the whole picture with Samsung Health. You can do a lot more with the fitness app than just set goals and see statistics. When using a Galaxy Watch, it is one of the most important applications. Plus, it works with any device with a screen, whether it's a smartwatch (any brand, not just

Samsung) on your wrist, a smartphone, or even a smart TV. Learn about the app's features and what makes it special.

How does Samsung Health work?

One such app that promotes physical activity is Samsung Health. The software, which is compatible with both iOS and Android devices, keeps tabs on your activity levels and other vital health metrics, allowing you to better understand your overall health. Additionally, Samsung wearables rely on it as their primary fitness app.

Keeping up with a healthy lifestyle is made easy with the Samsung Health app, even if it isn't the most feature-rich or complicated software out there. It keeps track of your food intake, your exercise objectives, your stress levels, and your sleep, all in an easy-to-understand format. Fitness instructors, mindfulness exercises, and a group of people who share your interests are just a few of the many services it provides.

Samsung Health monitors what?

A lot of the fundamentals are tracked by Samsung Health. You can manage your general health using this program, and it also serves as a repository for your most critical data. A user's activity level, sleep, heart rate, and number of steps may all be recorded alongside their exercises. You have the option to manually enter your sleep data or have Samsung Health automatically monitor it, depending on your device. Depending on the gadget, some fitness trackers may monitor your SpO2 levels, snoring, and the amount of background noise even while you sleep.

Samsung furthermore provides Sleep Coaching for users of the Galaxy Watch 4, 5, or 6 lines of smartwatches. By integrating data from your compatible watch into the Samsung Health app, the tech giant can deduce your sleeping habits. Approximately one week later, it will provide you with a sleep animal that symbolizes your routines. To help you get the most out of your sleep, the app compiles your data and then offers a coaching program that spans many weeks.

Calories, water consumption, and weight can all be monitored with this app. Depending on the device; the Samsung Health app may also monitor blood glucose levels, blood pressure, and blood oxygen levels in addition to heart rate and stress data. Finally, the app will record women's health information, such as menstrual cycles and symptoms.

Exploring the Samsung Health app and creating a profile

Your Samsung account is the login credential for Samsung Health. Get the app, then go to the "Create account" section and enter your information if you don't already have a Samsung account.

- Home, Together, Fitness, and My Page are the four primary tabs to explore once you've logged in.
- Within the Samsung Health app, you'll find your home base under the Home tab. Goals may be defined and tracked, and current health data can

be seen here. Weight, periods, food and drink consumption, and other data may be reviewed or entered manually by scrolling the Home tab.

- In the "Together" section, you may post challenges and see how your stats stack up against others. To help your friends stay inspired on their health journeys, you may also connect with others and invite them.
- Health: Use the Fitness option to get a 15-minute exercise video, a bedtime tale, or information about premenstrual syndrome. Workout programs, films, material from Samsung Health TV partners, mindfulness tools, and women's health resources are all part of the vast fitness and wellness library that can be found under this menu.
- Your Samsung Health app profile may be edited on the "My page" menu. To get useful information like calorie burn and heart rate range, enter your gender, height, weight, and birthday. In addition, you have the option to choose your usual degree of daily activity from one to four. Overview information such as personal bests, badges achieved, challenges, and weekly summaries are available under the My Page page, in addition to your basic profile.

Tap the three horizontal dots in the upper right corner of your screen to access the app's overflow menu from any of the tabs above. Extra choices are available on this menu:

- Take a look at the weekly summary of your recorded results, including your activity and sleep statistics, under the "For you" section.
- Advertisements and current sales on other Samsung items may be found in the "Promotions" section.
- Notes: Here you may discover announcements from the Samsung team, such as app upgrades and details regarding Samsung Health content.
- Configuration options: You can do all the usual stuff—view your privacy settings, control alerts, and access your account details—from this menu.

Creating and monitoring objectives

The Samsung Health app encourages users to establish a variety of health objectives. Establishing a target number of active minutes each day is the primary objective. Tracked steps, sports, and workouts all contribute one minute of moderate, mild, or strenuous activity toward this objective. A user may also set goals for monitoring their sleep, water consumption, body composition, steps taken, and calories consumed each day.

The many ways in which users may examine their monitored data is one of the app's strongest points, according to Samsung. Select a category (e.g., exercise, sleep, heart rate, etc.) from the Home tab to bring up a new screen that provides a more detailed analysis of your data. To see your results for the last week, month, or year at a glance, hit the calendar or bar graph symbol in the upper right-hand corner.

Galaxy Health-compatible applications

Several third-party applications, which Samsung calls "connected services," do not allow direct connectivity with Samsung Health, in contrast to competitors like Apple Health and Google Fit. Two notable outliers are the fitness platform Technogym and the widely used running and cycling app Strava. Nonetheless, Samsung's Health Connect feature does permit data synchronization.

Samsung Health-compatible devices

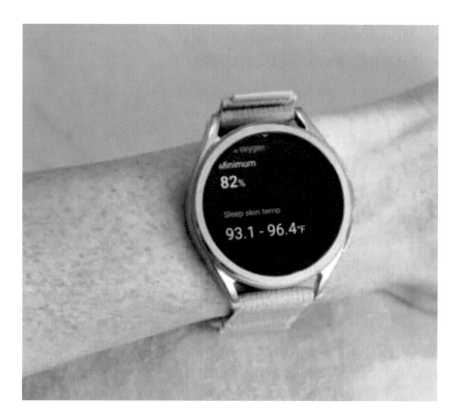

Samsung Health is compatible with a wide range of fitness and health gadgets, including many smartwatches from Samsung. To see all of the supported devices, go to the app's settings by tapping more (the three vertical dots in the upper right corner of the screen). You may peruse the gadgets mentioned in each category by scrolling down to Accessories and tapping on it.

The following fitness trackers, wrist watches, and accessories are Samsung Health compatible:

- Monitors for physical activity
- Fit, the Samsung Galaxy S
- Galaxy Fit e, Samsung Gear Icon X, and Samsung Galaxy Fit 2 (2018)
- Gear Fit from Samsung
- The Gear Fit 2 by Samsung
- Google Fit 2 Pro by Samsung
- The Urban-HR Patron
- Urban-S Plus: Partron
- Urban Partron-Pro
- Wearable computers
- Watch from Samsung Galaxy
- Android Wear smartwatch from Samsung
- Android Wear 2 from Samsung
- Galaxy Watch 3 from Samsung
- Galaxy Watch 4 from Samsung
- The Classic Samsung Galaxy Watch 4
- Android Wear 5 from Samsung
- The Galaxy Watch 5 Pro from Samsung
- Galaxy Watch 6 from Samsung
- The 6 Classic Samsung Galaxy Watch Model
- Gear S from Samsung
- Updated Samsung Gear S2
- Introducing the Samsung Gear S3!
- Products from Samsung

- The Samsung Gear 2 is arrived!
- Gear 2 Neo by Samsung
- Wearable device sensors from Samsung
- Two-sensor bike Computer from Garmin
- Garmin Heart Rate Monitor
- The following sensors are available: Garmin Speed, Polar Cadence, Pulse, and Polar Speed/Cadence for Cycling.
- Sky Blue Wahoo
- Cadence RPM Wahoo
- Woofer RPM Rate
- Various digital sensors for speed and cadence on the Trek Bontrager DuoTrak and DuoTrak S, as well as blood pressure monitoring
- The Transtek UA-651 BLE from A&D Medical is a blood pressure monitor.
- Glucose monitors from Omron, the BP7000, and the HEM-9200T
- Aviva Connect by Accu-Chek
- You may choose between the Accu-Chek Guide, the i-Sens CareSens NM Premier BLE, and the i-Sens CareSens N NFC. Smart glucose monitor GlucoNavii Link 0.3 NFC Smart glucose monitor GlucoNavii Mentor BLE SD The GlucoNavii Mentor NFC SD biosensor Blood sugar

monitoring devices from Sang Healthcare GluNEO M3
- This is the Garmin HRM.
- Hi-Run HRM-Garmin
- Fitbit Versa HRM-Tri
- Heart Rate Monitor by Garmin with a Comfortable Strap
- Heart Rate Monitor Belt with Gpulse
- Wireless Sports Headset by Jabra
- Polar H7 Activity Tracker
- Multisport Heart Rate Monitor by Suunto
- Heart rate monitor made by Suunto for their sports tracker
- 2.4-Amp Digital Heart Rate Monitor by Timex and Scosche Rhythm Plus
- Watch your heart rate with the Wahoo Soft ANT.
- Tickr by Wahoo Run by Wahoo
- Measurement devices
- Medical Devices by A&D UC-352 BLE
- Inside the human body, H20 (B, N)
- Omela Viva (HBF-222T) Lefu Smart Scale CF376
- Arctic Harmony Shinil SHM-D200AK
- Tanita BC-1000 (gray/white) Tanita BC-1100F, ANT+ Tanita BC-1000PLUS, and Tanita BC+ Tanita BC-1500+ANT
- The BF-2000 Tanita

- Ant Tanita HD-351
- Xiaomi Mi Smart Scale, Yunmai Color, Yunmai Mini, Yunmai Mini 2, and Yunmai Premium

To see statistics and exercises on a larger screen, you may also access Samsung Health on a compatible TV. This is a feature that many people love for their exercises at home. After you've logged into your Samsung account on the mobile app, you may connect it to your TV using the Samsung Health TV app.

A mobile app developed by Samsung for health tracking

For the most optimal experience, download the Samsung Health app to your phone. A larger screen, as opposed to a smartwatch, makes it much easier to see finer details. You may install the app on Samsung phones, Android 8.0 or later, and iPhone 5 and later running iOS 9. There is no support for Apple products, including the iPad and iPod Touch.

TIPS AND TRICKS FOR USING YOUR SAMSUNG SMARTPHONE

Contacts may be added and shared using QR codes.

Using QR codes, adding and sharing contacts on a Samsung mobile device is a breeze. You may make a QR code with your contact information and share it with others or scan another person's QR code by following these instructions.

Giving out your information

1. Launch the messaging app. Open your phone's Contacts app.
2. View your contact information. Find your personal contact information.
3. Hover over the QR code symbol. Find the QR code symbol in the lower left corner and press on it.
4. Distribute your QR code. A QR code for you has been created. Give this code to a gadget that needs it. The receiver may quickly add your contact information by scanning your QR code.

Integrating a contact

1. Launch the messaging app. Launch your phone's Contacts app.
2. Unlock the power of QR codes. On top, you should see a QR code symbol.
3. Look for the QR code. Scan the QR code on another smartphone while holding your device firmly.

4. Ensure that the new contact is saved. You may see your updated contact info when you scan the code. Put this in your contact list.

The following instructions will show you how to quickly and simply exchange your contact information via QR code and how to add new contacts to your phone by scanning the QR codes of other people.

Exchanging a misplaced mobile phone

Samsung With the free Find My Mobile service, which you can access via your Samsung account, you may remotely back up your data, find your registered Samsung Galaxy mobile device, and even erase all of its contents. Find My Mobile: Here's how to track down and handle your misplaced phone.

1. Establish the Find My Mobile service. Connect your Samsung device to Find My Mobile. Find, back up, and erase data from your registered Samsung smartphone using this free service.
2. Please provide the most recent whereabouts of your device. Use Find My Mobile to transmit your device's last known location if it becomes lost, assisting in its recovery.

3. Offline finding must be enabled. When your device isn't online, you may still find it by enabling Offline finding.
4. Use a remote to unlock your device. If you happen to lose your smartphone, you may unlock it remotely.
5. Find a misplaced handheld electronic gadget. To find out where your misplaced phone is right now, use Find My Mobile.
6. Keep tabs on your battery life and network connection from anywhere. View the status of the device's battery and network from a distance.
7. Dial up the ringtone. Turn up the volume on your gadget to its highest setting so you can hear it if it's close by.
8. Protect your gadget from accidental power-offs, show a contact number, or lock it. Make your smartphone more secure by locking it, making it impossible to power off, or showing a contact number on the screen.
9. Follow the whereabouts of your gadget. Use Find My Mobile to keep tabs on where your smartphone is at all times.
10. Rip data or create a backup. You may safeguard your information by remotely erasing data or backing up your device in case you are unable to access it right away.

11. Minimize power consumption. Utilize Find My Mobile to get advice on how to prolong the battery life of your handset.
12. Get into your smartphone even without a password or PIN. If you need to, you may unlock your smartphone without entering a password or PIN.
13. Find out the moment your gadget joins a network. Get alerts whenever your misplaced gadget establishes a network connection.

When you lose your Samsung mobile device, there are several options available via Find My Mobile to help you find it and manage it. The helpful service provides a full toolbox to handle the loss of your device, including locating it, protecting data, and making sure it is secure.

Using Samsung Wallet to add and use a card

Using Samsung Wallet is like carrying a virtual wallet. Here are the methods to add and access several types of cards on your Samsung mobile device: payment, membership, gift, digital key, health pass, digital asset, boarding pass, and more.

Integrating a card

1. Tap on the Samsung Wallet app. Go to the Galaxy app store and get the Samsung Wallet app, or open it.
2. Log in after you accept the permissions. After you've given the app the go-ahead, sign in using your Samsung account.
3. Define the process for verification. Pick one of two options: your fingerprint or your PIN.
4. Put a card into play. Find "Add" on the Quick Access tab and press on it.
5. Pick a method of payment. Press "Payment cards" next.
6. View card information via the camera. Take a picture of your credit card and add your billing data using your phone's camera.
7. The card was inserted with no issues. Samsung Wallet now has your card information.

Paying for something

1. From the main screen, swipe up. Pull up the menu from the main screen.
2. Choose a card. Pick out the payment method you'd like to use.
3. Analyze fingerprints. Authorize payment and confirm your identity with a fingerprint scan.

4. Pass the card reader over. At last, place your phone under the card reader at the checkout counter.

If you follow these instructions, adding cards to your Samsung Wallet and then using Samsung Pay to pay for things in stores will be a breeze.

Save time by pinning applications to your quick launch.

You may pin an app to your home screen so you can easily find it and use it anytime you need it. Follow these steps.

App pinning

1. Browse recently used applications. Press the "Recent apps" icon to start. You may get a rundown of all the applications that are open on your phone right now.
2. Choose an app to save. Select the app that you would want to save. Then, open the preview window and touch the symbol on top.
3. Under "Keep open," choose your selection. Choose "Keep open for quick launching" from the list of alternatives. By selecting it, you may "pin" the app so it stays open in the background.

4. Locked and pinned app. You can't exit the app after you've pinned it. Once the app has been securely pinged, you'll see a lock symbol.

Taking an app off the first page

1. Tell me which app is pinned. Find the app that has been pinned. Seek for the symbol of a lock.
2. Drop the app's pin. Just press the lock symbol to remove the app from the pin. This returns the app to its original condition.

Follow these steps to effortlessly customize your Samsung mobile device's experience and make your applications more accessible by pinning and unpinning apps.

Making printouts with your mobile device

Your Samsung Galaxy mobile device makes printing documents a piece of cake. To print documents using the integrated Office Mobile app, follow these steps to set up a print service.

Establishing a printing solution

1. Mobile app for Access and Office. Launch the desktop version of Office Mobile.

2. Find the print settings. Find the Options icon in the upper right corner of the Office Mobile app and press on it. Go to the menu and choose "Print."
3. Put in a printer. Select "Add Printer" from the menu that appears in the upper left corner of the screen. If your printer is not instantly recognized, choose "Add printer."
4. Choose a printing provider. From the list, choose a printer. Get the print service app for the printer you want to use, if you don't already have it installed.
5. Raise the printer's profile. Just add your printer when you install the print service app. Establish a direct connection by inputting the printer's IP address or using Wi-Fi.
6. Pick a printer. After that, choose the printer you just installed. Accepting the connection request could be necessary for your printer.

Putting your work on paper

1. Set the print settings. Set up the printer's print preferences once you've connected it. Modify the number of copies, choose a color scheme, define a desired range of pages, and much more.

2. Printing may begin. To start printing when you've adjusted your settings, touch the yellow print icon.

Printed materials in the future

When you want to use the same printer for another project, just choose your print settings and hit "Print."

With a few simple steps, you can use the Office Mobile software and the printer that comes with your Samsung mobile device to print documents.

Document scanning with your mobile device

Scanning and sharing documents is a breeze with Samsung Mobile. Here you will find detailed instructions on how to use the camera and the Office Mobile app to scan and distribute documents, whether they are single pages or many pages long.

Scan documents that are one page long

1. Launch the camera app. Start up your Samsung Galaxy phone's camera app.
2. Statement of purpose. Straighten up your camera's vision so that the document is in the middle.

3. Detection by itself. The camera app recognizes the paper without any user intervention. Press the "Scan" button after that.
4. Examine the scan. Press the thumbnail of the scan to examine it. Review the scan quality by zooming in.
5. Save your changes. To your liking, you may alter, trim, or rotate your scan. Press "Save" when you're done.
6. Spread the word. Select a method (email, Messenger, etc.) and then hit the share symbol to send the document to someone else.

Extracting text from many pages

1. Android and iOS applications for Open Office. The Office Mobile app may be accessed.
2. Convert the file to PDF format. Click on "Actions" located in the lower right corner of the screen. Hit the "Scan to PDF" button.
3. Page one is scanned. Make a quick scan of the cover page. Next, choose "Add New."
4. Look around more. Carry out the steps again for every page. Select "Done" by tapping the red arrow.
5. Evaluate and revise. Give your pages a once over. Resize them or add notes if you choose. After you're done, hit "Done."

6. Distribute the file. Next, send the scanned multi-page document in an email or upload it to Messenger.

Get more done in less time by scanning and sharing documents with your Samsung Galaxy mobile smartphone. Just follow these instructions.

Scan QR codes to add and share contacts

Using QR codes, adding and sharing contacts on a Samsung Galaxy mobile device is a breeze. Make a QR code with your information or scan another person's using these simple steps.

Making a unique QR code

1. Launch the Contacts app. Launch your phone's Contacts app.
2. Get in touch with us. The next step is to access your personal contact information.
3. Scan using a QR code generator. Press the QR code symbol located in the bottom left corner of the screen.
4. Quickly adding contacts. A fast and easy way for someone to add your contact information to their device is to scan your QR code.

Using a QR code scanner to import contacts

1. Launch the messaging app. Launch your phone's Contacts app.
2. Unlock the power of QR codes. Then, go to the app's main menu and touch the QR code symbol.
3. Use your smartphone's QR code scanner. Keep your phone steady while you hold it up to the QR code that contains the information you want to add.
4. Make sure to save the new contact. The information of the new contact is shown after scanning the code. Remember this person's contact information.

A quick and simple method to connect with new people on your Samsung Galaxy mobile device—just follow these instructions to make and share your personal contact data QR codes and to scan and store other people's QR codes.

Samsung mobile device mirroring smart TV

Screen mirroring makes it simple to project the contents of your mobile device onto a Samsung Smart TV, enhancing the watching experience on both devices. You may find the Smart View function on the majority of Samsung Galaxy mobile handsets. Let me show you how to fix it:

Casting your desktop image

What is needed:

- One that can reflect the display of another device
- The latest in intelligent mobile technology

Various companies may use different names for their screen mirror choices. Try to find words like:

- Display using wireless means of reflection
- Screen casting, mirror sharing, screen sharing, and multi-screening
- Smart View may be enabled in only three simple steps:

1. **Setting Up Smart View on Your Television**
   - Move to the Settings menu. On your Samsung Smart TV, go to the "Settings" menu.
   - Click on General. Opt for "General."
   - Manager for External Devices. Press the "External Device Manager" button.
   - Find the list of devices. Tap "Device List" after going to "Device Connection Manager."
   - Equipment that is currently accessible. When you press the screen, a list of connected devices will show up.
   - Decide on a system. Choose the name of your mobile device from the list.
2. **Turning on Smart View**

- Easy configuration. Draw down the panel for Quick Settings.
- Enhanced View. The Smart View icon may be found and tapped.
- Equipment that is currently accessible. To find other devices that are accessible to connect to, your device does a scan.
- Modern Smart TV from ID. Find and choose the "Samsung Smart TV."
- Toss in your queue. Just select "Start now" to begin casting with Smart View.

3. Permission to Pair Your Mobile Device

- With Your TV. You may see a permission request in the upper right corner of your screen.
- Give it a go. Click "Allow" to connect.
- Link up. See what's on your phone or tablet on the big screen of your Samsung smart TV.

With Samsung Smart View, you can enjoy all the content on your Samsung mobile device on a bigger screen. In little time at all, you will be screen casting if you follow these easy steps.

Combining your energy with that of another gadget

Wireless PowerShare is an in-built feature of Samsung mobile Galaxy devices that allows you to charge other Qi-certified devices wirelessly. Just stack the two devices on top of each other. You won't need a cable.

1. See how much juice is left in the battery. Before anything else, check that your battery is at least 30% charged.
2. Messages Regarding Access. Swipe down the Notifications panel until you see the "Wireless PowerShare" button; press it to activate PowerShare.
3. Message box for confirmation. When you are prepared to charge, a menu will display.
4. Switch the gadget off. Flip your gadget over so the display is facing down.
5. Arrange gadgets. Position two devices so that the middle of your phone is touching both of them.
6. Harmony with chi. Keep your Qi-enabled Samsung gadget or accessory charged. Many gadgets that aren't Qi-compatible with Samsung may nevertheless use it.
7. Connected or unconnected. When your Samsung Galaxy phone is charging or when you want to use it wirelessly, utilize Wireless PowerShare.

8. Take the gadgets apart. When the power transfer is complete or when the other device is completely charged, disconnect them.
9. Turn it off automatically. After 30 seconds of inactivity, Wireless PowerShare will turn off until it finds a second charging device.

Turn on Wireless PowerShare by following these instructions. Then, make use of your ability to share by charging another device while you're out and about.

Made in the USA
Thornton, CO
10/29/24 17:34:47

3d4db1bf-b3f7-4dd5-a53b-779dcb8b7c96R01